Determined to Stand and Fight

THE BATTLE OF MONOCACY
JULY 9, 1864

by Ryan T. Quint

EMERGING CIVIL WAR SERIES

Chris Mackowski, series editor
Kristopher D. White, chief historian

Also part of the Emerging Civil War Series:

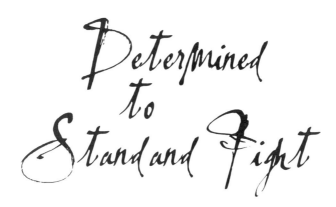

Determined to Stand and Fight

THE BATTLE OF MONOCACY

JULY 9, 1864

by Ryan T. Quint

EMERGING CIVIL WAR SERIES

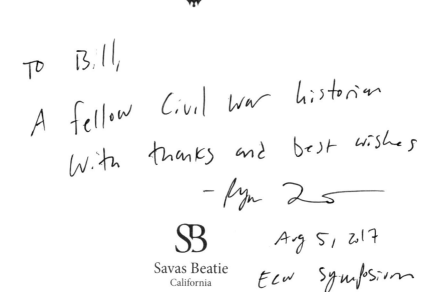

To Bill,
A fellow Civil War historian
With thanks and best wishes
— Ryan

Aug 5, 2017
ECW Symposium

SB
Savas Beatie
California

First edition, first printing

ISBN-13 (paperback): 978-1-61121-346-1
ISBN-13 (ebook): 978-1-61121-347-8

Library of Congress Cataloging-in-Publication Data

Names: Quint, Ryan T., author.
Title: Determined to stand and fight : the Battle of Monocacy, July 9, 1864 /
by Ryan T. Quint.
Description: First edition. | El Dorado Hills, California : Savas Beatie, 2016. | Series: Emerging Civil War series | Includes bibliographical references.
Identifiers: LCCN 2016042428| ISBN 9781611213461 (pbk) | ISBN 9781611213478
(ebk.)
Subjects: LCSH: Monocacy, Battle of, Md., 1864.
Classification: LCC E476.66 .Q85 2016 | DDC 973.7/37--dc23
LC record available at https://lccn.loc.gov/2016042428

SB Published by
Savas Beatie LLC
989 Governor Drive, Suite 102
El Dorado Hills, California 95762
Phone: 916-941-6896
Email: sales@savasbeatie.com
Web: www.savasbeatie.com

Savas Beatie titles are available at special discounts for bulk purchases in the United States by corporations, institutions, and other organizations. For more details, please contact Special Sales, P.O. Box 4527, El Dorado Hills, CA 95762, or you may e-mail us at sales@savasbeatie.com, or visit our website at www.savasbeatie.com for additional information.

MIX
Paper from
responsible sources
FSC
www.fsc.org   FSC® C011935

For Joanna

Table of Contents

Footnotes for this volume are available at
http://emergingcivilwar.com/publications/the-emerging-civil-war-series/footnotes

List of Maps

Maps by Hal Jespersen

Acknowledgments

PHOTO CREDITS:
W.F. Beyer and O.F. Keydel, *Deeds of Valor: Volume I* (wfb/ofk); Sarah Bierle (sb); Charles M. Blackford, "Thomas Jellis Kirkpatrick," *Virginia Law Register*, 1903 (cb); W. Asbury Christian, *Lynchburg and Its People* (wac); *Confederate Veteran Magazine* (cv); Department of Defense (dod); Jubal Early, *Lieutenant General Jubal Anderson Early, C.S.A., Autobiographical Sketch and Narrative of the War Between the States* (je); *Frank Leslie's Illustrated Newspaper* (fl); Fredericksburg & Spotsylvania National Military Park (fsnmp); Phillip S. Greenwalt (pg); Harpers Ferry National Historical Park (hfnhp); Nathan Harris, *Autobiography: The Story of an Old Man's Life with Reminiscences of Seventy-Five Years* (nh); James H. Hawley, *History of Idaho: The Gem of the Mountains: Volume II* (jh); E.M. Haynes, *A History of the Tenth Regiment, VT. Vols* (emh);

I would first like to express my love and appreciation to my family, who have always been supportive of my endeavors and journey. The week I graduated from college, my entire family came from Maine to Fredericksburg, Virginia, and then stuck around for a few days. While they were down, on one abysmally hot day we drove up to Monocacy to walk around the battlefield, and one of my of fondest experiences was next to the Worthington Farm, going through the motions of loading a 12-pounder Napoleon Cannon while my pre-teen nephews were all-too-happy to provide the accompanying sound effects.

Next I want to send along my ultimate gratitude to Chris Mackowski, editor of the Emerging Civil War Series and co-founder of the Emerging Civil War blog. In 2013, I was a summer intern for the Fredericksburg and Spotsylvania National Military Park, and on days when the two of us were stationed at the Wilderness Exhibit Shelter, between tours or on slow days, we just talked history. One day I brought an especially dog-eared and beaten-up copy of Glenn Worthington's *Fighting for Time*, and Chris was naturally curious enough to talk about the battle of Monocacy for a couple of hours—he served as my first sound board, bouncing ideas back and forth and playing devil's advocate.

The professors in the History Department at the University of Mary Washington and my colleagues at the Fredericksburg and Spotsylvania National Military Park have made me a much better historian.

This book would not have been possible without the help and support of the staff and volunteers at the Monocacy National Battlefield. They were always willing to go the extra mile on all of my research trips to their excellent archives. Please, go there and take advantage of the great resources.

Jake Wynn, Phil Greenwalt, and Avery Lentz all wrote excellent appendixes that make this a better book. Sean Redmiles and Sarah Bierle both allowed me to use some of their personal photographs of sites I couldn't personally make it to.

Ted Alexander, well-known and respected in the Civil War community, graciously agreed to write the book's foreword and reminds us that, while Monocacy may not have the fame of Gettysburg or Antietam, its human element is just as strong.

Kris White read the manuscript of this book with a sharp eye and offered many edits and suggestions that make it a better-finished book.

Hal Jespersen created the excellent maps that any book about a military campaign needs. He managed to take my chicken-scratch ideas and contortions and make them into maps that clearly show the battle's progression along the banks of the Monocacy River.

Finally, Joanna. She has been there with me, quite literally, every step of the way on this project. From helping research and making copies, to walking the battlefield and reading every word of this manuscript, I could not possibly thank her enough. Joanna, I love you, and this book is for you.

Historical Society of Frederick County (hsfc); Joseph Warren Keifer, *Slavery and Four Years of War A Political History of Slavery in the United States* (jwk); Osceola Lewis, *History of the One Hundred and Thirty-Eighth Regiment* (ol); Library of Congress (loc); Lovettsville Historical Society (lhs); Chris Mackowski (cm); Francis T. Miller, editor, *The Photographic History of the Civil War: Volume Three* (fm); Monmouth County Library (mcl); Monocacy National Battlefield (mnb); National Archives and Records Administration (na); National Museum of Civil War Medicine (nmcwm); *The National Tribune*, March 18, 1897 (nt); Naval History and Heritage Command (nhhc); *New-York Illustrated News*, July 30, 1864 (nyin); George Nichols, *A Soldier's Story of His Regiment* (gn); George Perkins, *A Summer in Maryland and Virginia or Campaigning with the 149th O.V.I.* (gp); Ryan T. Quint (rq); Sean Redmiles (sr); Alfred S. Roe, *The Ninth New York Heavy Artillery* (ar); Thomas Scharf, *History of Western Maryland: Volume I* (ts); Samuel Ward Stanton, *American Steam Vessels* (sws); Heber S. Thompson, *The First Defenders* (ht); U.S. Army Heritage and Education Center (usahec); Vermont Historical Society (VThs); Lew Wallace Autobiography, Vol. I (lw); Lew Wallace, "The Story of a Flag," *The Story of American Heroism*, 1897 (lw); *War of the Rebellion Atlas*, Plate 82 (wra); Frederick Wild, *Memoirs and History of Capt. F.W. Alexander's Baltimore Battery* (fw); John H. Worsham, *One of Jackson's Foot Cavalry* (jw); Jake Wynn (jw).

For the Emerging Civil War Series

Theodore P. Savas, *publisher*
Chris Mackowski, *series editor*
Kristopher D. White, *chief historian*
Sarah Keeney, *editorial consultant*

Maps by Hal Jespersen
Design and layout by H.R. Gordon
Publication supervision by Chris Mackowski

National Park Service
U.S. Department of the Interior
Monocacy
National Battlefield
NATIONAL PARK SERVICE

Foreword

BY TED ALEXANDER

When the subject of Monocacy comes up, I'm reminded of a trip my family took in the 1950s from the Pennsylvania border town of Greencastle to Frederick, Maryland. I was in elementary school but had already been bitten with the Civil War bug since a visit to Gettysburg in first grade. Our family's maternal roots were in Frederick County, Maryland, and this trip was to visit some cousins in Frederick, the county seat. Before meeting with them, we stopped in a local drug store. Back then it was the custom to sell picture postcards at such establishments. I noticed one postcard on the rack that featured a monument and cannon. Looking closer, I saw it was identified as Monocacy Battlefield. When we met with the cousins, I brought up the subject of Monocacy. My one cousin explained that it was not much to see: "Not like Gettysburg."

Indeed, it was and is "not like Gettysburg." In the 1890s, Gettysburg, Antietam, and other battle sites were being preserved by the United States War Department. But somehow Monocacy did not make the cut even though both Union and Confederate veterans pushed to have the site in rural Frederick County a "memorial park." When Congress finally got around to appropriating money for Monocacy, the funds were slashed drastically due to the Depression. Accordingly, the Congressional bill that was passed in 1934 established a battlefield with virtually no funding and no land.

Fast-forward to the 1980s. The National Park Service had taken over by the late 1970s and funds had been made available to purchase more than 1,500 acres of battlefield land. By the mid 80s, the

The familiar arrowhead of the National Park Service welcomes visitors at the entrance of the Monocacy National Battlefield. Behind the sign are arranged almost 2,200 flags—one for each casualty of the battle—that are laid out every Memorial Day weekend. (cm)

site was being developed for visitation. This effort included a visitor center featuring exhibits, a small electric map, and a book store.

The major thing missing was a book about the battle. At the time, I was serving as a consultant for a small book publisher in Pennsylvania. One of their goals was to reprint Civil War classics. In conversations with the noted historian, the late Brian Pohanka, he suggested we reprint *Fighting for Time* by Glenn H. Worthington. Originally published in 1932, Worthington was a local judge who, as a child, had witnessed the battle from his home on the battlefield. It was the only book-length study of Monocacy. The 1985 edition we published featured a new introduction by Pohanka along with additional battle accounts in the appendixes.

Since then, a number of books have been written about the bloody battle in July that probably saved the nation's capital. But I am proud to write the foreword to this new study by Ryan Quint in the popular Emerging Civil War Series. Ryan is an interpretive park ranger at Fredericksburg and Spotsylvania National Military Park. His skills as an interpreter translate to the well-written narrative of this book.

Ryan has a particularly good eye for incorporating both the strategic and operational aspects of what happened before and after the battle itself. He clearly points out the desperation of Confederate Gen. Robert E. Lee, who faced enormous odds before Richmond and eventually Petersburg, requiring him to send Gen. Jubal A. Early with a force of more than 10,000 men across the Potomac River into Maryland. There, in the last major Confederate incursion north of the river, the Confederates threatened the important logistics center of Harpers Ferry, and ultimately Washington, D.C., itself.

Like a scene out of an action movie, Early's advance was blunted just south of Frederick on July 9 along the Monocacy River. It was there that Union Maj. Gen. Lew Wallace gathered together a "pick up team" of troops of assorted combat efficiency. Augmented by veterans of the Army of the Potomac's VI Corps, they set forth to stop the Rebel juggernaut before it reached Washington.

For Wallace and his men, this was indeed an extreme challenge. Wallace was never able to muster more than 6,000 for the fight. Conversely, Early had around 15,000 veterans and more than 30 cannon, as opposed to the Union's seven guns. Yet, in a moment of high drama, the smaller Yankee force was able to buy time for the protection of the capital. That one-day delay along the Monocacy River was the critical moment of the campaign. For the numbers engaged and duration of the battle, it was a blood bath just as brutal as Antietam, Gettysburg, and other Civil War battles. After more than eight hours of combat, nearly 1,300 Union soldiers and around 1,000 Confederates became casualties.

So the question may be asked, "Why another book on Monocacy?" In *Determined to Stand and Fight*, Ryan Quint has provided us a good intro-level account of the battle. However, for the battlefield visitor who desires a quick understanding of why Monocacy was so important, Ryan's book is an excellent, concise study. Featuring more than 150 illustrations, the book is augmented with a number of appendixes covering medical care at the battle, the battle's impact on the civilian population, the ransom of Frederick, and the Johnson-Gilmor Raid on Baltimore. The latter event is an often-overlooked affair that really stands as one of the most spectacular mounted raids of the war. Two final appendixes examine the burning of Chambersburg on July 30, 1864, and the literary legacy of Lew Wallace, perhaps more famous as an author than a general for his book *Ben-Hur*. A driving tour of key battlefield sites and an overview of essential published studies on the campaign and battle round out this publication.

In retrospect, as my cousin pointed out on that warm day in Frederick almost 60 years ago, Monocacy was "not like Gettysburg." Indeed, the battle carries its own legacy that stands alone and equals Gettysburg in the ferocity of its combat and in its strategic importance in relation to the rest of the war.

Congratulations to Ryan Quint for providing us with an excellent study of an important and sometimes ignored campaign and battle of the American Civil War. Also, many thanks to the Emerging Civil War group for publishing another fine volume in their battle and campaign series.

For more than thirty years, Ted Alexander served as a historian with the National Park Service, most notably at Antietam National Battlefield. He is also the founder of the Chambersburg Civil War Seminars. In 2016, he was the inaugural recipient of the Emerging Civil War Award for Civil War Public History.

"I therefore decided to turn down the Valley and proceed according to your instructions to threaten Washington and if I find an opportunity—to take it."

—*Lt. Gen. Jubal A. Early, CSA*

"These men died to save the National Capital, and they did save it."

—*Maj. Gen. Lew Wallace, USA*

...E OF MONOCACY

· BONE · VOLVNTATIS · TVAS · CORONASTI · NOS · SCVTO · 1632

THAT SAVED WASHINGTON

THE BATTLE...
FOR WHILE...
ON WASHING...
GENERAL...
FROM...
OF WASH...
ATTACK...
THE...

Near Monocacy Junction

PROLOGUE

JULY 9, 1864

The bullet entered Pvt. George Douse's face, blowing out the back of his cheek and then striking the young Vermonter in the right shoulder. As some of his comrades carried Douse back to the picket line's reserve, Douse's skirmishing partner, Pvt. Daniel B. Freeman, remained on his own.

Freeman ducked down into the rifle pit he and Douse had dug, throwing dirt up against the iron rails of the Baltimore & Ohio Railroad. All around Freeman, rifles cracked as the 75 picked men of the 10th Vermont, paired with about 200 men of the 1st Maryland Potomac Home Brigade, skirmished and traded shots with the rebels across the fields from them.

The opposing forces were positioned about three miles south of Frederick, Maryland. Behind the Union skirmish line wound the Monocacy River,

OPPOSITE: Numerous soldiers on both sides at the battle of Monocacy paused before the action began to consider the natural beauty of the river valley—something visitors can still do as they walk the battlefield and ponder what happened there. (cm)

RIGHT: This perspective looks towards the National Park Service's visitor center. On July 9, 1864, these fields were filled with skirmishers and battle lines. Confederate forces would have moved towards the camera, with Federal soldiers deployed behind the camera. (cm)

Eighteen-year old George Douse survived his gruesome facial wound at Monocacy, recovering and living until 1914. (mnb)

and on the opposite banks of the river stood the rest of the Federal forces, getting ready to also enter the battle. Outnumbered and outgunned, the Federal soldiers had to stand and fight for the very defense of Washington, D.C. Only about fifty miles away from the firing line, Washington was a city in turmoil—with few troops ready to defend the capital's defenses. The fight shaping up along the banks of the Monocacy would be a holding action for the Union troops—some may even say a forlorn hope—delay, delay, delay. If they ran, the road would be wide open to the nation's capital.

But such lofty ideals were probably far from Daniel Freeman's mind at the moment. The fire from the Confederates was extremely close, he remembered even years later. He slid his rifle through some rails to fire, but the shot gave away his position. "I could not raise my head but a bullet would strike the rails in front," he wrote, "and one bullet struck the stock of my gun, one went through my blouse and another through the top rail inflicting a slight scalp wound."

So it continued for hours, Freeman firing and ducking down to reload. He bit the ends of cartridges, poured gunpowder, rammed the bullets home, and thumbed percussion caps onto firing cones. Over, and over, and over. "I fired upwards of 100 rounds," Freeman wrote matter-of-factly.

Sometime after Douse's wounding, Cpl. John Wright ran over to Freeman. The two of them were to move over, helping another Vermonter hard-pressed by the Confederates' skirmishers. Freeman left behind his familiar rifle pit, running alongside Wright to their new position. "As Wright and I reached this outpost," Freeman wrote, "Wright straightened up to take a view of the surroundings and was killed—shot through the head."

Picking Wright up, Freeman and the other Vermonter carried the corpse back to the rear of the picket. There, as they laid Wright down, sheltered for a moment by a contour of ground, an officer asked if anyone would go back to where Wright had just died to resume skirmishing with the Confederates. Freeman thought, and "after a moment," said he would.

So the Vermonter shouldered his rifle and ran back to the firing line.

With his skirmishing partner wounded, Daniel Freeman found himself alone for most of the afternoon, trading shots with an overwhelming number of Confederates. Wounded at the third battle of Winchester in September 1864, Freeman took this image without a left boot for his pension file. (na)

The Shenandoah Valley

CHAPTER ONE

From the beginning of the war, both sides understood the importance of Virginia's Shenandoah Valley. Ranging some 200 miles and nestled between the Blue Ridge and the Allegheny Mountains, the Valley had a common moniker as the "Breadbasket of the Confederacy"—providing badly needed victuals to Confederate forces.

Federal war efforts focused on denying the use of the Valley to their Confederate foes. Federal officers also hoped to use the avenues of advance deep into the heart of Virginia that the Valley offered. And yet, for all that strategic value, Union war leaders always seemed to put second-tier officers in charge of Federal forces sent to the Valley. This series of missteps began in the war's first campaign, when the Federal high command failed to keep Confederate troops in the Valley from leaving to support the Confederate effort in their victory at Manassas.

The worst failure, though, came in 1862. As Maj. Gen. George B. McClellan brought the largest army in the nation's history up the Virginia Peninsula, a bewildering set of incompetent generals were run ragged by Maj. Gen. Thomas "Stonewall" Jackson. Like knocking over dominoes, Jackson defeated the Federal officers—men like Nathaniel P. Banks, who lost so many supplies that the Confederates referred to him as "Commissary Banks," and John C. Fremont, who was a better

The Shenandoah River, which flows north from the valley it derives its name from, joins with the Potomac River at Harpers Ferry. (cm)

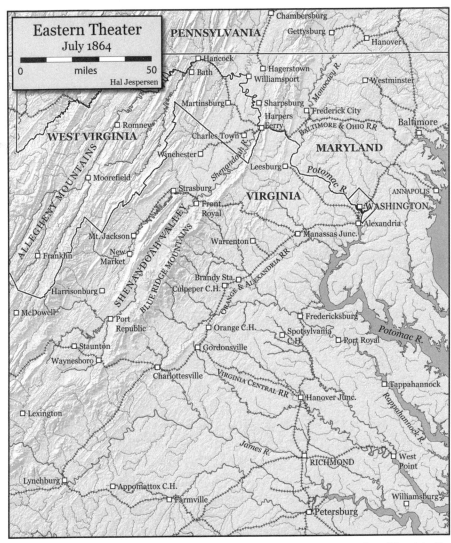

EASTERN THEATER—In 1864, Virginia saw military campaigns in nearly every section of the state. For the Confederacy, retaining railroad hubs like Lynchburg and Petersburg was a strategic necessity. Federal forces hoped to wrest control of the Shenandoah Valley away, something Jubal Early set out to stop.

explorer than soldier. Jackson's victories in the Valley made him internationally famous and left officials in Washington, D.C., fearing a move north. Thousands of Union soldiers, earmarked for McClellan on the Peninsula, instead stood guard elsewhere, watching for Jackson.

More defeat in 1863—this time at the Second Battle of Winchester—a loss that opened the door for the Confederate invasion of Pennsylvania and led to Gettysburg. It seemed that no matter how many troops the Union high command sent to the Valley, Confederates sent them stumbling back in retreat.

Lieutenant General Ulysses S. Grant hoped to change that. Coming east in the spring of 1864, Grant had no intention of allowing the Confederacy the freedom to maneuver troops around, shuffling men about to one endangered point after another. Before this spring, Federal armies had all operated in independent campaigns rather than in concert with one another; the Army of the Potomac's strategic goal varied widely from that of the Army of the Tennessee, which varied from the Army of the Cumberland, and so on. Grant, however, planned differently.

The armies would operate as one. They would time their Spring 1864 offensives together, striking the Confederacy with a wide sledgehammer that stretched from the familiar battlefields of Virginia, down to the mountains of Georgia and the rivers of Louisiana. As the general-in-chief of the United States Army, every soldier answered to Grant, and he intended to wield that power.

As the Federal high command tried to strip away the Shenandoah Valley from the Confederacy, they were met by Thomas "Stonewall" Jackson, who bewildered his foes in a lightning-speed campaign in the spring of 1862. (loc)

Promoted to lieutenant general in early 1864, Ulysses S. Grant came east to oversee the 1864 campaign. He would make his headquarters with the Army of the Potomac but would simultaneously keep an eye on the other armies operating elsewhere. (loc)

While Grant came into the field, Maj. Gen. George G. Meade still officially commanded the Army of the Potomac. The two men strained under the confines of the campaign, not aided by the failures in the Shenandoah Valley. (loc)

Gen. Robert E. Lee prepared his Army of Northern Virginia to face off against the Grant-Meade duo. Lee would also issue the orders that set the 1864 invasion of Maryland underway. (loc)

In Virginia alone, Grant planned four campaigns. The Army of the Potomac would square off with Robert E. Lee's Army of Northern Virginia with a new objective. No longer would the largest Federal army target Richmond, the Confederacy's capital but, rather, Lee's men themselves. "Lee's army will be your objective point," Grant told Maj. Gen. George G. Meade, the Army of the Potomac's commanding officer, "Wherever Lee goes, there you will go also."

Grant planned the rest of the Virginian operations as such: Richmond would be Maj. Gen. Benjamin F. Butler's target. Landing to the south of Richmond at Bermuda Hundred with his Army of the James, he would cut through the underbelly of rebel defenses. In southwestern Virginia, relative newcomers Brig. Gen. George Crook and Brig. Gen. William Averell were to cut the rail lines there, destroying them, preventing any further use.

And, for the Shenandoah Valley that had proved so troublesome for the Union war effort since the very beginning, Grant gave the reins to Maj. Gen. Franz Sigel. Sigel was tasked with finally neutralizing the Valley's ability to feed and nourish Confederate forces, and to prevent Maj. Gen. John C. Breckinridge's Confederates from reinforcing Lee once the combat began. It was an objective that left the onus for the heaviest fighting with Meade and Butler. When Grant explained his plans, President Abraham Lincoln summed them up as only he could: "Those not skinning can hold a leg."

The campaigns began in May, and almost immediately, Sigel ran into trouble. He delayed and hesitated, unsure and unconfident of his troops' ability to fight. For every bit of momentum Sigel gave, Breckinridge gladly took. Their climatic battle came on May 15, outside of the small town of New Market. In the midst of a driving rain storm, Breckinridge and Sigel's forces traded volleys and canister. Capped by a charge of the cadet battalion from the Virginia Military Institute, Breckinridge's men shattered Sigel's lines and sent the Federals retreating back towards the mouth of the Valley

Franz Sigel, a German immigrant to the United States in the late 1840s, had the task of capturing the Shenandoah Valley. Sigel's movement through the Valley quickly fell apart. (loc)

and their base of operations, Harpers Ferry, West Virginia. Another defeat was added to the resumes of Federal officers in the Shenandoah Valley.

* * *

Following Sigel's defeat at New Market, Maj. Gen. David Hunter took control of Federal forces in the lower Shenandoah Valley. Because the Shenandoah River flows in a northern direction, terminology for the Valley is a little different from what one may expect. To follow the river north meant to "go down the valley"—meaning that the Northern head, near Harpers Ferry, was the "lower Valley"—while to march south meant one went "up the Valley." Hunter's immediate goal was to march up the Valley and capture Lynchburg, a city that provided crucial railroad ties from southwest Virginia back towards the center of the state.

Within fifteen days of Sigel's defeat at New Market, Hunter had gathered the pieces of Sigel's force, reformed them, and set out for the upper Valley. Left behind, Sigel now oversaw the Reserve Division of the Department of West Virginia, a command no one honestly expected anything of but which would become vitally important within a matter of weeks.

As Hunter moved up the Valley, Confederate forces attempted to stop him. The Southern forces were hampered by the fact that Breckinridge, the victor of New Market, had been called with his forces towards Richmond. As Grant and Meade relentlessly pushed Lee, the Confederate commander desperately needed more men and so called on Breckinridge. While Breckinridge's men helped Lee at the battle of Cold Harbor, their absence was sorely missed in the Valley. Small skirmishes broke out between the two sides before the first pitched battle of Hunter's tenure, the battle of Piedmont, on June 5. Hunter won the battle, opening the rest of the Valley to his forces.

David Hunter intended a new strategy for the Shenandoah Valley—absolute destruction.

Sigel's column up the Shenandoah Valley came to a grinding halt at the hands of Maj. Gen. John C. Breckinridge. Breckinridge, a former vice president of the United States, beat Sigel at the battle of New Market and would go on to be second-in-command of the invading force sent into Maryland. (loc)

Following Sigel's defeat at New Market, Maj. Gen. David Hunter replaced him. A radical Republican, Hunter sought to not only defeat the Confederacy but to punish its people. Hunter introduced a hard-war approach to the Shenandoah Valley, burning as he went. (loc)

A radical Republican and staunch abolitionist, Hunter had little patience for secessionists, whether they be soldiers or civilians. Fighting for the Union and abolition, Hunter had already been wounded before—as a present for his 59th birthday, a Confederate riflemen shot him in the face at the First Battle of Bull Run. His decision while a commander in South Carolina to arm freed slaves made him infamous throughout the Confederacy and an outlaw in the eyes of Confederate President Jefferson Davis. Now, as he made his way south through the Valley, Hunter left a trail of desolation.

The onset of the greatest destruction came on June 11, when Hunter's force reached Lexington, Virginia. As the home to the Virginia Military Institute (VMI), whose cadets had recently taken part in defeating Sigel, Hunter would not let Lexington off easy. The day after his arrival, Hunter let his troops loose. A 16-year-old girl living in Lexington wrote that the Federals immediately targeted the military college. "Sunday morning about 10 o'clock the Yankees set fire to the Institute, blew the walls down and destroyed the mess hall and professors' houses. . . . All the Point property except the miller's and toll houses were burned." Federal forces also put to the torch the home of John Letcher, former governor of Virginia.

After four days of remaining in Lexington, Hunter collected his troops and continued South. Only forty-five miles remained between him and his objective at Lynchburg.

It had become readily apparent that Confederate help was needed in the Valley. After beating Sigel, John C. Breckinridge moved most of his command east, towards Richmond, to help Robert E. Lee against Ulysses S. Grant. Now Breckinridge hurried back to the Valley to face off against Hunter. While Breckinridge's men served as the vanguard, it became readily apparent that other troops would be needed as well.

Robert E. Lee, who believed Hunter "infested the Valley," chose one of his most dependable commanders, Lt. Gen. Jubal Anderson Early, to deal with the problem. One of the most well-known Confederate commanders, the irascible general and his Second Corps were almost 130 miles away from Lynchburg, fighting against the Army of the Potomac near Cold Harbor on the outskirts of Richmond. But no matter the distance, Lynchburg and its crucial rail lines *had* to be saved. Early received orders from Lee on June 12 to "strike Hunter's force in the rear, and, if possible, destroy it," as Early recounted years later. So his men, battered from fights at the Wilderness, Spotsylvania Court House, North Anna River, and Cold Harbor, boarded trains and headed towards their newest fight at Lynchburg.

Hunter arrived outside Lynchburg before Early. Confederate forces ringing the hills of the city would need to hold on for as long as possible—a move Hunter aided by underestimating his foes. Delaying in front of the city, Hunter threw away precious hours, letting more and more Confederate reinforcements arrive. Soon, his underestimation turned to fear, as the shrieking whistle of arriving trains in Lynchburg cowed Hunter from further movements. Even without reinforcements, Confederate commanders in Lynchburg deployed psychological warfare, bringing empty trains into the city, whistles blowing and troops cheering the boxcars as if they were filled to the brim with newly-arrived troops, convincing Hunter he was vastly outnumbered.

The opposing forces clashed for two days, June 17-18, filling the air with the rolling crackle of musketry and large clouds of dirty-white smoke that hung around the hills of the city. Hunter's

Hunter's trail of destruction reached its zenith on June 11, 1864, at Lexington, Virginia. In response to its cadets' participation in the battle of New Market, Hunter ordered that the Virginia Military Institute be put to the torch. (fm)

Federals retreated in the darkness of June 18, leaving behind a battlefield dotted with close to 1,000 casualties.

The Federals moved back in the night towards Liberty (now Bedford, Virginia), the sound of creaking wagons and tramping soldiers competing for noise dominance. The difficult maneuver of retreating in the face of the enemy, Chief of Staff David Hunter Strother happily recounted, "was well conducted and successful." A scathing Louisianan soldier wrote differently, however: "Hunter tucked his tail and ran like a wolf."

By sunrise of June 19, a final Confederate attack went forward, hoping to catch their foes unaware. But as the gray-and-butternut-clad troops charged, screaming their daunting rebel yells, they found empty positions where the day before Federal battle lines opposed them. Word soon raced back and the pursuit was on.

* * *

Early sent a dispatch to Lee on June 19, telling his commander of the victory at Lynchburg, and soon the Confederate forces chased after Hunter's retreating column. It was a foot race—Early had to get to Hunter before the Unionist general reached the safety of the screening Blue Ridge Mountains.

The race tested the strength of both forces. Strother, once so full of self-congratulation over the successful retreat from Lynchburg, just three days later wrote, "Worn out with fatigue, without supplies in a country producing little at best and already wasted by war, the troops are beginning to show symptoms of demoralization" as Confederate cavalry snipped at the column's heels. But the Confederates, too, were worn down, as Early wrote later with a touch of the Lost Cause pathos he was famous for: "there was a limit to the endurance even of Confederate soldiers."

In the end, Hunter won the race. His men made it to Buford's Gap and escaped over the Blue Ridge Mountains. Early's pursuit had failed to destroy Hunter's defeated Federals.

But Early had other plans to turn his mind to. As his corps had raced towards Lynchburg before their climatic showdown, he sent a telegram to Maj. Gen. John C. Breckinridge. "My first object is to destroy Hunter," Early telegraphed matter-of-factly, but the following line surely caused Breckinridge intrigue, "and the next it is not prudent to trust to telegraph."

Now that Hunter was defeated, what was Early's next step? He continued to hold his cards close to his chest, writing to Lee on June 22 that his troops were resting their weary feet but then tomorrow, "will move in accordance with original instructions."

What were the "original instructions" Early had from Lee? Hunter was defeated, yes, but Lee was currently battling against the Army of the Potomac at the gates of Petersburg, another vital railroad hub for the Confederacy. Was Early to remount his men on trains and bring them back east?

No. Early's men instead slung their blanket rolls over their shoulders and began to march North on June 23. It wasn't until Early was in Staunton, 75 miles north of Lynchburg, that he finally confirmed his intentions and orders with Robert E. Lee. "I therefore decided," Early wrote to his commander, "to turn down the Valley and proceed according to your instructions to threaten Washington and if I find an opportunity—to take it."

The Shenandoah Valley, designed only to be supplementary to Federal military operations, "holding the leg," as Lincoln called it, had suddenly become so much more than that.

After his stop in Lexington, Hunter turned his column towards Lynchburg, seen here in an 1853 print. Lynchburg had key railroad connections to southwestern Virginia and needed to be protected. Robert E. Lee looked to send a force under newly promoted Lt. Gen. Jubal Anderson Early (above) to defend Lynchburg. Early took the remnants of the Army of Northern Virginia's Second Corps and linked up with Breckinridge's forces. Early's victory at Lynchburg not only saved the city but sent David Hunter over the Blue Ridge into West Virginia. The road north was wide open. (wac) (loc)

The March North

CHAPTER TWO

LATE JUNE 1864

As he moved North, Jubal Early reformed his forces and retitled his command the Army of the Valley District. Marching with Early were some of the best combat troops the entire Confederacy had to offer in 1864.

The high standards started with Early himself. Born in Virginia in 1816, Early went to the Military Academy at West Point, graduating in 1837 (but not before a dispute that saw future Confederate general Lewis Armistead smash a plate over Early's head), and then serving with the 3rd U.S. Artillery. Early fought against the Seminoles in Florida and took part in the Trail of Tears, the forced removal of Cherokee Indians. Resigning from the army in 1838, Early entered law, but returned to service at the outbreak of the Mexican War in 1846, serving until the war's conclusion in 1848.

With the sectional crisis splitting the country in 1860, Early went to Virginia's secession debates as a Unionist, but when the Old Dominion seceded in the wake of Fort Sumter, Early threw his lot in with his state. He commanded a brigade of infantry at the war's first big battle, First Bull Run, starting a combat record with the Confederacy that saw him fight at nearly every major battle in the war's Eastern Theater.

By late June 1864, Early had only commanded the Second Corps for about a month because its previous commander, Richard S. Ewell, was forced to

This monument to Stephen D. Ramseur's North Carolinians stands not far from the infamous "Bloody Angle" at Spotsylvania Court House. Speaking of heavy fighting on May 12, 1864, it stands as a reminder of the type of experienced forces that Jubal Early brought north with him in the summer of 1864. (rq)

One representation of the average infantryman in the Army of Northern Virginia during the summer of 1864. He has rid himself of all but the necessitates, wrapping spare clothes and personal belongings in a blanket roll over his shoulder. (jw)

take medical leave because of debilitating dysentery. Though short on tenure as corps commander, Early still had an impeccable reputation as a hard fighter, and an equal reputation for profanity. "Very rough in language," one Confederate described, Early was a "great swearer and curser." Because of the temper and profanity, Lee referred to Early as his "bad old man." Harsh arthritis and rheumatism that stooped Early also certainly made him look much older than 48 in the summer of 1864. To his soldiers though, Early was "Old Jube."

Those soldiers were the ones that Early now depended on to threaten Washington, D.C. Early reformed them for the campaign, but it would be a hard task. The spring campaigns of 1864 played havoc with the Army of Northern Virginia's ranks—the Second Corps entered the campaign's first battle at the Wilderness with some 17,000 men but now could only muster about 8,000 muskets. It is not totally clear how many men Early took with him down the Valley, although estimates range from between 16,000-20,000. Besides the Second Corps's three infantry divisions, Early had Breckinridge's one infantry division, four brigades of cavalry under the command of Maj. Gen. Robert Ransom, and thirty-five pieces of artillery headed by Brig. Gen. Armistead Long.

For his infantry, Early decided to split the four divisions, keeping two as independent commands and putting the remaining two divisions under an ad hoc corps commanded by Breckinridge.

Major Generals Robert E. Rodes and Stephen D. Ramseur commanded Early's independent divisions. Both commanders were extremely experienced, having steadily risen through the ranks of the Army of Northern Virginia. Both of their commands, however, had been whittled down to almost nothing—numbering more in the range of brigades than divisions. Even with their small numbers, Rodes and Ramseur would prove strong subordinates for Early.

Breckinridge, James Buchanan's vice president, hailed from Kentucky. Serving as a senator for his state at the outbreak of war, Breckinridge needed to pick sides as the war got underway—a decision not as clear-cut as it had been for Early because Kentucky did not secede. Breckinridge threw his lot in with the new Confederacy, earning an official condemnation from the U.S. Senate: "Whereas John C. Breckinridge, a member of this body from the State of Kentucky, has joined the enemies of his country, and is now in arms against the government he had sworn to support . . . Resolved, That said John C. Breckinridge, the traitor, . . . hereby is, expelled from the Senate." Breckinridge fought for the first half of the war in the Western Theater, seeing action at Shiloh, Stones River, Chickamauga, and Chattanooga, before transferring to Virginia.

Lt. Gen. Richard Ewell had commanded the Second Corps through the opening stages of the Overland Campaign, but dysentery forced him to relinquish command to Jubal Early. He would oversee Richmond's defenses for the rest of the war. (loc)

For the time being, Breckinridge continued to command his own division, although Brig. Gen. John Echols would assume leadership near the Potomac River, leaving Breckinridge to oversee the corps. Echols's command was destined to miss the entire battle of Monocacy, while Breckinridge's other division, made up of Maj. Gen. John B. Gordon's three brigades, were fated to be in the heaviest and bloodiest fighting on the field.

In a war where the overwhelming number of generals came from military academies, John Brown Gordon serves as a notable exception. Hailing from Georgia, Gordon had absolutely no military experience when the war began, starting his service as captain of the "Raccoon Roughs," a company in the 6th Alabama. Like Rodes and Ramseur, Gordon also rose through the ranks, bearing the scars to prove it as well: at the battle of Antietam in September, 1862, Gordon was shot an astonishing five times. In the aftermath of the battle of Spotsylvania Court House, where the Second Corps fought in the horrendous Mule Shoe and its infamous Bloody Angle, Gordon was given command of a reorganized division of infantry containing, amongst others, the Stonewall Brigade and Louisiana Tigers. At one time some of the best troops in the entire Army of Northern Virginia, the Stonewall Brigade and Tigers now were mere

Two of the best division commanders in the Army of Northern Virginia, Maj. Gens. Robert Rodes (left) and Stephen Ramseur (right) were both ready for whatever orders Early had for them. They both commanded independent divisions, whereas Early's other infantry commands were folded into a corps under Breckinridge. (fsnmp)(fsnmp)

shadows of their former selves as a result of the bloodletting in the Overland Campaign.

In a similar fashion to Breckinridge's corps of infantry, various experiences and combat roles awaited Maj. Gen. Robert Ransom's cavalry division. While the Confederate troopers skirmished extensively in the days prior to the battle, only one of Ransom's four brigades of cavalry—Brig. Gen. John McCausland's—would see action at Monocacy. Ransom, while just as experienced as his infantry commander cohorts, was "in bad health ever since leaving Lynchburg" and resigned soon after the upcoming campaign.

Deciding factors in the action to come were the guns under the command of Brig. Gen. Armistead Long. Overseeing three battalions of artillery, encompassing nine batteries, Long wielded immense firepower on any battlefield. Trained artillerists from Virginia and Georgia manned the guns.

As Early moved his men north, Federal forces left them unopposed in the last days of June. Because Hunter had retreated through the Blue Ridge, he managed to take himself entirely out of the campaign for the foreseeable future. "I was glad to see Hunter take the route to Lewisburg," Early later wrote in his memoirs, "as I knew he could not stop short of the Kanawha River, and he was, therefore, disposed of for some time. Had he moved to Southwestern Virginia, he would have done us

Breckinridge's infantry commanders, Maj. Gen. John B. Gordon (left) and Brig. Gen. John Echols (right). Gordon would see the heaviest fighting at Monocacy; Echols would see none. (loc)(loc)

incalculable mischief, as there were no troops of any consequence in that quarter, but plenty of supplies at that time. I should, therefore, have been compelled to follow him."

*   *   *

Just because the Confederates were unopposed, their movement was by no means a secret. On June 29, the telegraph line clacked back towards Washington, D.C. "I find from various quarters statements of large forces in the Valley," the telegram started. "Breckinridge and Ewell are reported moving up. I am satisfied the operations and designs of the enemy in the Valley demand the greatest vigilance and attention."

The man responsible for sending the telegram was not an officer in the Union army, but rather, a civilian. John W. Garrett served as president for the Baltimore & Ohio Railroad (B&O), a line that ran from Baltimore to Parkersburg, West Virginia. It proved a critical connection to the central United States, and Garrett worried what a Confederate force could do to it.

Garrett's warning, however, went unheeded. In Washington, Chief of Staff Henry W. Halleck sent along the warning to Grant, then at City Point, near Petersburg, Virginia. "There are conflicting reports about the rebel forces in the Shenandoah Valley. Some say that Breckinridge and [George E.] Pickett are following the cavalry . . . while others say they are not in the Valley at

Not feeling well, Maj. Gen. Robert Ransom would resign soon after the coming campaign. His cavalry brigades screened Early's movement north, but he was personally a non-entity in the coming battles. (fsnmp)

LEFT: Brig. Gen. Armistead Long commanded the 35 or so cannon that Early brought north. Long's gunners would dominate the battlefield at Monocacy, helping to push back Federal forces. He would also serve as Robert E. Lee's military secretary. (loc)

RIGHT: President of the Baltimore & Ohio Railroad, John Washington Garrett worried about the safety of his tracks and was left unsatisfied with the Federal high command's seemingly apathetic reaction to word of Confederates marching north. He sought help elsewhere. (mnb)

all. It certainly would be good policy for them (while Hunter's army is on the Kanawha) to destroy the [B&O], and make a raid in Maryland and Pennsylvania."

An hour and a half after getting Halleck's message, late at night on July 1, Grant replied that Early's "corps has returned here [Petersburg], but I have no evidence of Breckinridge having returned."

With Grant disregarding the notion of a substantial Confederate force in the Valley, Early's men had more time to operate unopposed. Not until July 2, when Early's vanguard reached Winchester, Virginia, 165 miles north of Lynchburg, did they meet resistance from Federals. But the small Federal cavalry unit in Winchester quickly retreated, leaving the city that changed hands the most during the war to experience yet another transition back to Confederate control.

That Federal cavalry belonged to Franz Sigel, the disgraced commander from New Market who now led the Reserve Division out of Harpers Ferry, West Virginia. "There are strong indications of a movement of the enemy in force down the Valley. Our cavalry met those of the enemy to-day at Winchester," Sigel wrote to Washington, joining Garrett's choruses of warnings.

Still, Grant did nothing, even replying adamantly two days later, "Early's corps is now here," again meaning Petersburg. "There are no troops that can be threatening Hunter's department," Grant insisted.

Looking down Shenandoah Street at Harpers Ferry offers a glimpse back in time. (cm)

Finally, John Garrett had had enough. Nearly a week had passed since his first warning, and nothing had been done. Ulysses S. Grant and Henry Halleck both horribly managed the opening of Early's campaign against Washington, a trend that would continue in the days to come. Realizing he was getting nowhere with the military's top brass, Garrett decided to see someone else.

He would pay a visit to Maj. Gen. Lew Wallace.

Lew Wallace

CHAPTER THREE

EARLY JULY 1864

About three miles south of Frederick, Maryland, on the western bank of the Monocacy River, the B&O had a railroad junction. Freight and passengers from Baltimore could either continue along the main line, heading to West Virginia, or take the turn and move towards Frederick. To get to the junction from Baltimore, however, a train had to cross an iron bridge that spanned the Monocacy, a winding river that local American-Indian tribes had called the Monnockkesey or Menachkhasu—translated, depending on the source, as "river with many bends" or "'fortified' (i.e., *fenced, a garden*)" [emphasis in original].

In 1862, during the Antietam campaign, Confederates came to Frederick and targeted the B&O bridge, destroying the center span in hopes of preventing Federal reinforcements from Baltimore. It had cost the B&O in excess of $11,000 to fix the destroyed bridge, so in 1864, John Garrett was not so keen on having a repeat performance by marauding Confederate soldiers. No one knew where the Confederates under Early were headed, but Garrett preferred to not take any chances.

Sources are not exactly clear about when Garrett visited Major General Wallace's Baltimore headquarters, but it likely came on July 2. In his unfinished autobiography, Wallace recalled

The railroad bridge that crosses the Monocacy today had its platforms built in the 1870s at the same site as the railroad bridge that John Garrett wanted defended in 1864. (cm)

Garrett's bridge over the Monocacy River had already been destroyed once before. During the Maryland Campaign in September 1862, Confederate forces had blown the bridge apart, forcing thousands of dollars in repairs. (loc)(loc)

Garrett's "calls as significant of important business, bracing myself accordingly."

Today, Lew Wallace is best known for authoring the monumentally bestselling *Ben-Hur: A Tale of the Christ*, but in 1864 that book was still sixteen years in the future, and Wallace was struggling to find his place. The 37-year-old major general from Indiana was not West Point trained, instead climbing through the ranks because of natural ability. He had served as a young teenager in Mexico in the late 1840s, and, although he had not seen any combat, still loved the martial lifestyle. As the son of an Indiana governor, Wallace was well connected when the Civil War broke out. First as a colonel, then a brigadier general, Wallace proved himself capable of command, most notably at the battle of Fort Donelson, in February 1862, along the Cumberland River in Tennessee. Moving to the endangered right flank of the Union line without orders, Wallace earned a major general's second star on his shoulder, becoming the youngest—at 34, to attain the rank in the Union army up to that time.

That upward projection came to a screeching halt at Shiloh almost two months later. Encamped away from Ulysses S. Grant's main field army, Wallace's division received orders to move to the right flank, near Shiloh Church, on the morning of April 6. Wallace's route to the battlefield remains controversial to this day with a common assertion that he became lost. This is an incorrect assertion—not for a second was Wallace ever lost at Shiloh. But Wallace's star was soon tarnished by his commanding officers.

Looking for scapegoats, both of Wallace's superiors at the time, Maj. Gen. Henry Halleck and Grant, pinned blame elsewhere for the high casualties that shocked the country. Halleck hated Lew Wallace for the simple fact that Wallace had never attended an official military academy (Halleck, in fact, hated anyone without that trait, which he thought a fundamental prerequisite to commanding troops in the field). In the days after Shiloh, Halleck blamed the Union army's high casualties on "bad conduct of officers who were utterly unfit for their places." This not-so-subtle jab was aimed at men like Wallace—officers with no formal military background.

For General Grant's part, he believed Wallace had been promoted above his ability. Grant approached the situation passive-aggressively, leaving the post-Shiloh writings to his staff officers, many of whom zeroed in on Wallace, blaming him for not getting to the battlefield in time. Leaving Grant's army, Wallace did not help his own situation by testifying in front of a Congressional committee. Pivoting blame back towards Grant and Halleck,

Garrett visited the Eutaw House Hotel, where Maj. Gen. Lew Wallace rented out several rooms as headquarters for the Middle Department. The hotel burned down in 1912 and is now the site of the Hippodrome Theatre, which opened in 1914. (loc)

Maj. Gen. Lew Wallace had served as the commander of the Middle Department/ VIII Army Corps since March 1864. Garrett's call for help would be his first chance for major action since a series of unfortunate events that started at the battle of Shiloh on April 1862. (loc)

Wallace criticized the lack of any pursuit of the defeated Confederates after Shiloh: "I waited for those orders and waited; but they never came. Why they did not, I do not know, nor did General Grant ever tell me."

The word-sparring continued in the summer of 1863, when Wallace asked for a poorly-timed court of inquiry into the Shiloh matter, still wanting to present his case against Grant and Halleck. Grant had just captured Vicksburg, opening the Mississippi River to total Union control, and frankly no one cared what Lew Wallace thought or did. Halleck punctuated that philosophy by replying to Wallace's request: "I do not think that Genl. Wallace is worth the trouble & expense of . . . a court of inquiry . . . His only claim to consideration is that of gas." Wallace meekly withdrew his request but continued to look for ways back into the fight as he sat on the proverbial sidelines.

In March, 1864, just one-month shy of the two-year anniversary of Shiloh, Wallace received new orders. They did not give him a combat role, but rather command of the Middle Department, headquartered in Baltimore. Overseeing land in four separate states, it was an administrative job, whose main responsibility consisted of keeping the genteel of Baltimore—a city that had been a thorn in the side of the Union war effort—happy. Even that was too much in Halleck's opinion, who complained, "It seems but little better than murder to give important commands to such men as. . . Wallace, and yet it seems impossible to prevent it."

The luster of the position soon wore off, and Wallace grew bored, bemoaning the fact that he would miss yet another campaign, and thus the military glory that came with great battles.

And then John Garrett came.

Garrett explained the situation and wanted Wallace's help. It seemed, Garrett said, that not only did no one seem to grasp the importance of Early's movements through the Valley, but also, if Early was truly moving up for the purpose of invading Maryland, just how unprepared Baltimore or Washington were to defend themselves. "You know," Garrett stressed, "there are no troops at Washington—at least not much more than enough to enable . . . to keep the peace in the city?"

Wallace understood well the predicament. As Grant pushed continuously south during the Overland Campaign, casualties piled higher and higher. To replace them, he stripped cities like Washington and Baltimore of their defenses, mainly consisting of "heavy artillerists" who had sometimes trained for years on handling the cities' big cannon. Giving the artillerists rifles, Halleck shipped the soldiers south by the thousands to fill the thinning gaps in Grant's infantry lines.

As the commander of the Middle Department, Wallace technically commanded the VIII Army Corps, but calling his force a corps was being overwhelmingly generous. The troops numbered, at most, about 3,200 men, and most of them were 100-day enlistees. Named for their terms of enlistments—only about three months—the soldiers were designed to take the place of the garrisons heading South. One such Ohioan in Wallace's command later wrote that the transitions allowed some units, "2200 strong, as fine a body of men as I ever saw" to be "sent to the front," while in their place remained, "800 Ohio hundred day men."

Wallace's command for the time being consisted of a mix of troops: two Ohio National Guard units and a Maryland infantry battalion, all three serving as 100-day units, as well as two traditional three-year regiments, and an artillery battery. These men

Commanding a division of infantry at Shiloh, Wallace was accused of getting lost on his way to the Shiloh battlefield. It was a false accusation, but Federal high command continued to blame Wallace, especially because of his status as an officer with no formal military education. Wallace spent the rest of his life trying to clear his name. (loc)

Chief of Staff Henry W. Halleck was Wallace's political foe during the Civil War. For all of his bias against Wallace, though, Halleck's performance during Early's campaign through Maryland left much to be desired. (loc)

meant well, but even Wallace described them years later in relation to the rebel veterans they would soon have to fight as "inefficients."

Similar commands now defended Washington—and it was no secret. In the same message to Lee describing his planned march North, Early assuaged his commander, "I hear there is nothing at Washington but the same kind of men," meaning 100-day militia units that had never seen combat.

The defenses of the city took on increased significance in the summer of 1864, separated only by a matter of a few months from the presidential election in November. Although no Democratic candidate had been chosen yet—that would not come until August with George B. McClellan's platform—if Early could threaten the capital, it would improve the chances of pro-peace Northerners who favored an end to the war at any cost. Abraham Lincoln already faced turmoil in his own party and administration, and any bid for re-election would be all but crushed if Early managed to get into Washington.

It would be a Herculean task for the 100-day units to face off against Early, but with Grant and Halleck all but asleep at the wheel of command, someone had to act. The nation's capital lay all but undefended, and without any action, Early would march straight in unopposed. In his autobiography, Wallace dramatically recounted his reply to Garrett's plea for help in defending the iron railroad bridge. Likely written with his novelist's touch, embedding a touch of fiction, the lines still read dramatically and portend what Wallace's decisions led to in the coming days:

> *"It is very clear," I said, "that your iron bridge over the river at the Monocacy Junction is essential to communication with Harper's Ferry, and as I have a block-house, with two guns in it, on the eastern bank covering the bridge, I will assume guardianship of the structure from my end of it to the other. You may take with you my promise—the bridge shall not be disturbed without a fight."*

*   *   *

The day after Garrett's visit, Wallace began to set his troops in motion. While Wallace stayed in Baltimore, he sent orders to his direct subordinate, Brig. Gen. Erastus B. Tyler. Tyler had seen plenty of action, even fighting against Jackson in the Shenandoah Valley in 1862, but the gruff veteran was another officer who had seemingly been exiled to the Middle Department. His feud did not come with someone as high as Grant or Halleck but rather the Army of the Potomac's Chief of Staff, Andrew Humphreys, who levied charges of misconduct against Tyler for actions during the battle of Fredericksburg in December 1862. Though acquitted for most of the charges Humphreys threw at him, Tyler was still an unwelcome figure in the Army of the Potomac's hierarchy.

Brig. Gen. Erastus Tyler served as Wallace's second-in-command within the Middle Department. Tyler had served ably in the Shenandoah Valley as well as at Fredericksburg and Chancellorsville before he, too, made political enemies of his own in the Union army's command structure. (na)

Tyler's initial orders from Wallace read to deploy the 3rd Maryland Potomac Home Brigade (PHB). Wallace doubted that the single unit of infantry would be enough, and because of this, Tyler's orders continued, "if necessary push . . . any other available troops forward to Monocacy Junction"—a stipulation Tyler soon exercised. In Baltimore, the mobilization of the artillerists of Frederick Alexander's local battery ended the "good time had so near home, where we could go three or four times a week, and get a square meal, have a good bath and change clothes, go to the theatre and other amusement," as the battery's historian noted years later. The gunners got to watch the July 4th fireworks over Baltimore—one last treat of home—before having to make their way to the Monocacy.

Other units also prepared to head towards the Monocacy and the railroad bridge, units including the newcomers, the Ohio National Guards. "[W]e received orders to be ready to take the [trains] in 30 minutes with 3 days [sic] rations . . ." one of the guardsmen wrote. "Not having any provisions cooked, we filled our haversacks with hard tack and raw sowbelly."

As Wallace and Tyler pulled their troops together, no one yet had a clear picture of what exactly was coming North. Mystery and confusion zipped through the telegraph lines from Harpers Ferry to Baltimore and Washington, D.C. On Independence Day, July 4, Grant still insisted that "If General Hunter is in striking distance there ought to be veteran force enough to meet anything the enemy might have." He even sent orders for Hunter that, when he arrived, he was to take command of the whole operation against whatever Confederate force may be in the area. Such orders were impractical, however; Hunter was still in the Kanawha, and it would be days before he arrived back in the theater of operations. And then, as Grant continued to depend on Hunter's arrival from West Virginia, the telegraph lines west of Frederick went dead. "Telegraphic communication cut west of Frederick," Tyler reported from the Monocacy River. From Harpers Ferry to Frederick, a distance of almost thirty miles, was now dead space.

"[T]he front which I had thought myself too far behind for any disturbance was swinging my way and demanding my presence," Wallace wrote in his memoirs. He sent a request to Garrett: prepare a personal train for him.

Wallace may have been overly dramatic in his postwar reminiscences, but at the time, even he did not have a full grasp of the situation as it was unfolding, as suggested by his wife, Susan, writing from his Baltimore headquarters. "Lew buckled on his sword saying he would go down to Point of Rocks (the extreme limit of his Department) and look after a gang of guerillas there, would be back day after tomorrow," she wrote, adding, "Once there he found things more serious than he expected."

Wallace grabbed one aide, Maj. James Ross, and immediately after midnight of July 5, made his way to Camden Station. He hopped aboard a waiting engine and sped off towards the Monocacy River.

One of the most iconic stadiums in Major League Baseball, Camden Yards is home to the Baltimore Orioles and is near the spot where Lew Wallace climbed aboard a train to make his way to the Monocacy River. The famed warehouse at the stadium was built in 1899. (sr)

Sigel Delays at Harpers Ferry

CHAPTER FOUR

JULY 3-6, 1864

Today Harpers Ferry is best known for abolitionist John Brown's raid, hoping to spark a slave insurrection, against the Federal armory in October 1859. Quickly put down, Brown's insurrection and subsequent execution made him a martyr to the cause of abolition and provided yet another spark to the tumultuous years leading up to the outbreak of war. Now Federal soldiers routinely went into battle singing "John Brown's body lies a-mouldering in the grave,/ But his soul goes marching on."

Located at the conflux of the Shenandoah and Potomac Rivers, Harpers Ferry, West Virginia, offered strategic avenues of approach for both sides. A Union force marching south could follow the Shenandoah like a dagger into the heart of the Valley; along the Potomac, a Confederate force had a clear shot towards Washington.

On July 3, a day after first making contact with Federal forces in the lower Valley, Early's men broke camps and continued marching north. Their objectives were the two Federal depots at Martinsburg and Harpers Ferry; capturing both would net them a wealth of provisions as well as scattering any opposition capable of slowing them down.

Looking down from the summit of Maryland Heights, one can soon see how the high ground dominated Harpers Ferry and allowed Federals to deny Jubal Early's intentions. (sb)

John Brown (above) brought national attention to Harpers Ferry, then part of Virginia, when he attacked the Federal arsenal there in October 1859. When Brown's raid started to fall apart, he positioned himself in the engine house of the arsenal (top right), where United States Marines attacked and captured him. He was executed less than two months later. (loc)(rq)

Major General Franz Sigel, commanding at Martinsburg, knew Early's men were on their way. He tried to gather as many of the supplies as possible and send them back down the track towards Harpers Ferry, even as his outposts began to make contact with Early's vanguard. By the late afternoon of July 3, telegraph lines were clacking with reports of "severe fighting" at Martinsburg. The B&O operator in Martinsburg made his way out of the town as the Confederates closed in and reported back to Baltimore that, Sigel's attempts notwithstanding, "Not more than one-half of the Government stores was removed. . . . Most that left is forage." Sigel knew he had no choice but to pull his small force out of the town, abandoning the left-behind supplies to the incoming Confederates. Sigel marched his men to Shepherdstown and its crossing points over the Potomac River. As he crossed the river late on the hectic July 3, Sigel telegraphed a subordinate, Brig. Gen. Max Weber, another *immigré* commander, at Harpers Ferry. "I shall march to Harper's Ferry at 2 a.m. to-morrow" Sigel told Weber.

Weber spent July 3 trying to get a response from Washington, D.C. He begged Halleck that night: "I need infantry very much." The following day, Independence Day, Weber again tried to raise a response from Halleck, bemoaning, "I have but 400

Franz Sigel commanded at Martinsburg, West Virginia. As Early's troops closed in, Sigel ordered out as many trainloads of supplies he could, then retreated towards Harpers Ferry. (loc)

men" but then also reiterating, "I shall not leave the town, except at the last necessity."

As the Federals tried to prepare for the Confederates, Early's men moved in. On July 3, Early had split his force, sending Maj. Gen. John Gordon's division towards Martinsburg while Rodes's and Ramseur's divisions marched on Harpers Ferry. By July 4, those two division commanders closed in on the Federal positions. Weber scattered his small force throughout the town, with some of his troops positioned at Bolivar Heights while Union artillery protected the infantry from the dominating Maryland Heights. Ramseur and Rodes deployed skirmishers, and soon the air filled with the sharp crackle of rifles and musketry. Looking back at the fighting around Harpers Ferry, one civilian remembered, "At no time during the war was there as deep a gloom on Harper's Ferry as on that anniversary of the birth of our nation."

The fighting on July 4 around the town went quickly as Confederate numbers soon overwhelmed Weber's force. "No regular line of battle was engaged in the attack," wrote Thomas Wood, a

Born in the Germanic state of Baden in 1824, Max Weber graduated from a military academy and, soon after, joined forces in the Revolution of 1848, serving under Franz Sigel, the same man he would cooperate with in 1864. Weber fled Europe in the aftermath of the failed revolution and settled in New York, where he joined the Federal army when the Civil War began. (loc)

soldier in Rodes's division, "but our sharp shooters drove the enemy from Bolivar, and part of the town of Harper's Ferry, capturing thereby quite a quantity of Commissary stores, even a plenty of luxuries." The Confederates were all too happy to seize the stores, and Wood continued, "How strange to see 'Confeds.' with cigar, sugar, coffee, lemons, whiskey, and everything which the most fastidious soldier could desire." The looting of supplies at Harpers Ferry by Confederate forces became one of the most talked-about incidents of the whole campaign, with one Georgian remarking that they "consumed" the spoils "and continued the celebration by a considerable display of fireworks— or firearms" and pushing the Federals further back.

The July 4 celebrations went on at Martinsburg, as well, with one Georgian scribbling, "the yankes dident know that we was every whers. . . . Busy they were fixing up for a grate Juberlee goin to give a Big Diner Barbacure. They had every thing that could mention."

At Harpers Ferry, Weber's heavy cannon, most notable a 100-pounder Parrott rifle, continued to fire into the town as the Confederates celebrated their luxurious spoils. Jedediah Hotchkiss, Early's topographer, described the fire as little but a nuisance, "doing little damage." Even if the Federal artillery fire was more bark than bite, Jubal Early grew unsure of his troops' combat readiness at both Martinsburg and Harpers Ferry. As they continued to loot, he tried to stress that "It is absolutely necessary that the most rigid discipline be enforced, else disgrace and disaster will overtake us." There was still fighting to do—made all the more difficult on the night of July 4-5 when Weber decided to give up the entirety of Harpers Ferry and instead retreat up the high bluffs of Maryland Heights.

As Weber's beleaguered force made their way up the Heights, they were joined by Franz Sigel's column from Martinsburg, so that by morning of July 5, the Federals had about 6,000 men safely ensconced behind fortifications, looming overhead of Harpers Ferry. Sigel's men brought with them 26

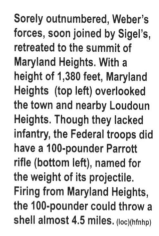

Sorely outnumbered, Weber's forces, soon joined by Sigel's, retreated to the summit of Maryland Heights. With a height of 1,380 feet, Maryland Heights (top left) overlooked the town and nearby Loudoun Heights. Though they lacked infantry, the Federal troops did have a 100-pounder Parrott rifle (bottom left), named for the weight of its projectile. Firing from Maryland Heights, the 100-pounder could throw a shell almost 4.5 miles. (loc)(hfnhp)

pieces of artillery that joined Weber's battery and the 100-pounder Parrott.

Sigel and Weber's occupation of Maryland Heights pivotally changed the campaign. Before, Jubal Early's men had seemed unstoppable, marching as juggernauts and gaining momentum with each day. But as daylight came on July 5, that momentum came to a stop. Throughout the war, Harpers Ferry seemed like a hot potato, constantly changing hands between the opposing armies. Most famously, Stonewall Jackson captured the town and its large garrison in 1862 by capturing Maryland Heights after a lackluster defense by the Union commander. With his guns imposed against the town, Jackson easily forced Harpers Ferry's capitulation. Now, almost two years later, the Federals would not give up Maryland Heights so easy. Thomas Wood, who had written about the "Confeds" with cigar and lemonade, noticed the contrast: "Jackson had taught the Yankees that Maryland Heights was the key to Harper's Ferry," he wrote, "and since its first capture they had made the position quite formidable."

A quick capture of Harpers Ferry and its access to the Potomac River would have given Jubal Early a straight approach to Washington, D.C. But with Sigel and Weber literally above him, he hesitated. Early later admitted, "My desire had been to manoeuvre the enemy out of Maryland Heights, so as to enable me to move directly from Harper's Ferry for Washington; but [the Federals] had taken refuge in his strongly fortified works . . . and an attempt to carry them by assault would have resulted in greater loss than the advantage would justify."

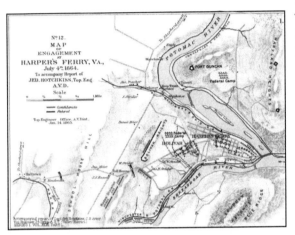

Jedediah Hotchkiss, the famed cartographer for Stonewall Jackson earlier in the war, continued his map-making skills for Jubal Early. His map for the action at Harpers Ferry shows the skirmishing through the town and the defensive Union positons atop Maryland Heights. (wra)

With his original plan to move down the Potomac River ruined by the Federals atop Maryland Heights, Early needed to change his strategy. He sent out orders to his infantry commanders to swing back towards Shepherdstown, cross the Potomac River, and move towards the Heights from behind, hoping to evict Sigel and Weber. Crossing the Potomac River, many of the troops spent the night of July 5-6 near the old Antietam battlefield where reminders of the war's bloodiest day hounded the soldiers. Captain Robert Park of the 12th Alabama jotted in his journal, "Memories of scores of army comrades and childhood's friends, slain on the banks of this stream, came before my mind, and kept away sleep for a long while."

Sigel and Weber remained atop Maryland Heights, the heavy artillery hammering away at the Confederates maneuvering around the town below them. On July 6, John B. Gordon's division closed in on the heights from the Maryland side, hoping for one last chance to push the Unionists off. For the next two days, July 6-7, Gordon's men engaged in a series of skirmishes that produced a tremendous amount of smoke and noise, but few casualties. "Throughout the whole of this day [July 7]," one report from Gordon's division read, "there was heavy skirmishing along the line and continued cannonading—Loses very light."

Though the losses may have been "light," they still parried Early's last attempt to capture Maryland Heights. The lieutenant general thus changed his plans—he would move his army north to the South Mountain passes and then move into the Monocacy River Valley. From there Early hoped to reach the Georgetown Pike, and, as he wrote to General Lee, "I then move on Washington." But Early's intended move through Frederick would bring him directly towards Lew Wallace.

*　　*　　*

On July 3, as the garrisons of Martinsburg and Harpers Ferry prepared for Early's men to arrive, Maj. Gen. Henry Halleck continued to telegraph Lt. Gen. Ulysses S. Grant outside of Petersburg. In an ironic case of those living in glass houses throwing stones, Halleck besmirched the command abilities of Sigel, Weber, and other Federal officers there. "You can . . . judge what probability there is of a good defense if the enemy should attack the line in force," Halleck spat.

Confederate soldiers bivouacked on the old Antietam battlefield on July 5-6, 1864. Memories flooded many of the Confederate soldiers of the fighting on September 17, 1862, that left almost 23,000 dead, wounded, and missing—the bloodiest single day in American history. (loc)

Ordered to detach troops from his VI Corps, Maj. Gen. Horatio Wright (left) chose Brig. Gen. James B. Ricketts (right). Ricketts had seen plenty of action, being wounded and captured at the battle of First Manassas in July 1861, and commanding infantry at the battle of Antietam. (loc)(loc)

But as the besieged troops atop Maryland Heights fought to a standstill, Grant and Halleck *finally* began to stir. On July 5, a full week after John Garrett's first warning, Grant at last admitted from Petersburg, "I think now there is no doubt [Early's] corps is away from here." That same afternoon, Grant sent orders to Maj. Gen. George Meade to "Send in one good division of your troops," in order to reinforce the garrisons at Harpers Ferry. The orders made their way to Maj. Gen. Horatio Wright, commanding the VI Corps, just after midnight the next day, July 6.

Left to pick which of his three divisions would go, Wright chose Brig. Gen. James B. Ricketts's 3rd Division, totaling some 4,000 men. As Wright sent orders to Ricketts, a second note arrived from Meade's headquarters: "No artillery will accompany the division that is to embark" for Harpers Ferry. Leaving behind the trained and veteran gunners in the corps' batteries was a decision the Federal high command would soon have reason to regret.

Ricketts's veterans were awoken early on July 6 with orders to march from their works outside Petersburg to the wharfs at City Point where steamers waited to take them to Baltimore. The march brought the men through mounds of dust so that, by the time the division reached City Point, the chaplain of the 10th Vermont Infantry remembered that the New Englanders were "so completely covered with dust that we were mistaken for a division of colored troops." Another of Ricketts's

men wrote that because of the swirling dust kicked up by marching feet, "we could not see 20 feet from our selves, this added to the heat was dreadful."

Once at City Point, the soldiers embarked on the waiting ships and made their way down the James River and towards the Chesapeake Bay. The soldiers appreciated the change of scenery, with Lt. George Davis remarking that they were "thankful for rest, pure air, and to be beyond the reach of shot and shell" for the first time since the opening of the spring's bloody campaigns in May.

The soldiers of James Ricketts's division did not know it, but they would soon be embroiled in some of the bloodiest fighting along the banks of the Monocacy.

After a hard and dusty march from their trenches at Petersburg, Ricketts's troops arrived at City Point, where they loaded onto steamships like this, the *Daniel Webster*. Built in 1854, the *Daniel Webster* was originally designed to be a passenger ship between Boston, Massachusetts, and Bangor, Maine. It carried from Ricketts's division the 10th Vermont and part of the 106th New York Infantry towards Baltimore. (sws)

First Contact

CHAPTER FIVE

FREDERICK, MARYLAND, JULY 7-8, 1864

At Monocacy Junction, Maj. Gen. Lew Wallace continued preparing his troops. With Brig. Gen. Erastus Tyler serving as his second-in-command, Wallace managed to wrangle together three regiments of Maryland infantry, two of Ohio National Guardsmen, the battery of Baltimore Light Artillery, and some mounted Ohioans—a motley collection to be sure. Wallace was not exactly assuaged of his worries for defending the bridges over the river, later characterizing some of the inexperienced troops as "unexceptional."

Late on July 6, though, arrived Lt. Col. David Clendenin with his 8th Illinois Cavalry troopers. Technically not assigned to Wallace's department, Clendenin nonetheless agreed to stay on and offered the use of his experienced troopers. The Illinoisans had spent the past couple of days sparring with famed rebel partisan, Col. John S. Mosby, around Point of Rocks on the B&O Railroad.

Early the next morning, Clendenin brought his roughly 230 troopers towards Middletown, about ten miles west of Frederick. With the newly arrived veteran troops, Wallace wanted to reconnoiter and find out exactly where Jubal Early's vanguard was. The troopers were joined by two 3-inch rifles from Cpt. Frederick Alexander's Baltimore Light

The fields where fighting occurred west of Frederick on July 7 and 8 are completely urbanized. An interpretative sign from the Civil War Trails placed on the fringe of a parking lot discusses the skirmishing in the two days prior to the battle of Monocacy. (rq)

Lt. Col. David Clendenin brought experienced cavalry troopers with him to the Monocacy River, something Wallace desperately needed. In 1865, Clendenin served on the same commission as Wallace trying the conspirators in the Lincoln Assassination trials. (mnb)

Lt. Peter Leary served as the second-in-command of the Baltimore Light Artillery. After the Civil War, he stayed in the United States Army, serving out west and retiring as a brigadier general. When he died in 1911, he was the last surviving officer of the Baltimore Light Artillery and was buried in Arlington National Cemetery. (fw)

Artillery—the section commanded by Lt. Peter Leary—while Alexander remained behind with the remaining pieces. Moving up the Hagerstown Pike, the Illinoisans and Baltimoreans crossed through the Catoctin Mountain while the sun climbed higher into the sky, growing to be "very oppressive," the 8th Illinois's historian remembered.

Ahead of Clendenin's small force lay the pickets of the Loudoun Rangers, a small, pro-Union outfit raised in Virginia. As dawn came, the Virginians ranged forward, getting closer to Middletown. The Unionists ran smack into Early's vanguard, the cavalry brigade of Brig. Gen. Bradley T. Johnson, a native of Frederick, and whose men now deployed for action just ten miles from his home. Heading Johnson's column were the troopers of the 1st and 2nd Maryland Cavalry, led by Maj. Harry Gilmor, another Maryland native.

As the two sides opened fire, an interesting set of circumstances unfolded: pro-Union Virginians fought against secessionist Marylanders, who, despite their state's official loyalty to the United States, now fought for the Confederacy.

Gilmor brought up more Confederates, maneuvering through the streets of Middletown and opening up such a fire that one Loudoun Ranger described it as "a tornado over our heads," thus forcing the Federals to fall back towards Catoctin Mountain. "We fell back in good order," before meeting Clendenin's force at the mountain pass, the Rangers' historian wrote.

Clendenin and his troopers would hardly have agreed with that historian's summation. "The Loudoun Rangers are worthless as cavalry," Clendenin wrote, while the Illinoisans' historian said that the Virginians "had run back into [Frederick] at the first sight of a grayback."

Having left Frederick around 5:30 a.m., Clendenin didn't hit Johnson's Confederates until shortly after 10 a.m. He fanned his troopers out while Lt. Leary's cannon continued firing. On the other side of the firing line, Bradley Johnson brought more cavaliers up to contest the ground

Looking down the Old National Pike that runs through Middletown; in the distance rises South Mountain. On July 7, Confederate cavalry units came down the mountain passes towards the camera's perspective, pushing Federal cavalry units back. (rq)

between Middletown and Catoctin Mountain. Gilmor's brother, Richard, became a casualty when one of Leary's shots sent shrapnel into his leg and scattered the other rebels nearby.

For five hours the opposing troopers traded carbine fire while the artillery banged away. One of the Federal shells exploded as a company from the 8th Virginia cavalry deployed into line, killing ten and wounding another eight. The horrific aftermath left one hospital steward stunned. "Since the beginning of the war," he wrote, "I have seen death in many of its horrid forms but never so frightful a wound" as from that shell.

With mounting Confederate pressure, Clendenin moved back, re-crossing the Catoctin. As he did, he came upon Col. Charles Gilpin, commanding the 3rd Potomac Home Brigade and another of Alexander's rifled-guns. Turning command of the force over to Gilpin, Clendenin stayed with the troops as they closed in on the western fringes of Frederick. "The gallant troopers of the Eighth never did better fighting than this," the Illinoisans' historian asserted—a strong endorsement considering some of these troopers had fired some of the first shots of the battle of Gettysburg a year earlier.

Bradley Johnson's Confederates followed their opponents closely. While he made his headquarters at John Hagan's tavern on the road to Frederick, Johnson ordered some of his own artillery up to try help dispel the Federals. From the roof of his home,

A 1903 reunion of surviving members of the pro-Union Virginia cavalry unit the Loudoun Rangers. The Rangers were all but wiped out later in the war fighting against Col. John Mosby's Confederate partisans. (lhs)

prominent Frederick resident Jacob Engelbrecht watched the two forces spar. The Confederate gunners dropped the tails of their pieces "about a mile from town," Engelbrecht wrote. "They then commenced throwing shells & balls." The noise attracted a number of other civilians who "ventured as near as it was prudent to see the skirmishing."

Having fallen back to the outskirts of Frederick, Colonel Gilpin's Marylanders and Lieutenant Colonel Clendenin's Illinoisans skirmished with Johnson's Confederates until nightfall. Gilpin ended the night's fighting with one last push with some of his companies, forcing out dismounted rebel troopers. With darkness limiting visibility, the two sides separated, "with a seemingly mutual understanding that it would be renewed in the morning," as one *New York Times* reporter noted.

Brig. Gen. Bradley Johnson led the way with Confederate cavalry, clearing Middletown and moving on Frederick. A native of Frederick, Johnson found himself embroiled in sectional strife even before the Civil War started: in 1857, he caned prominent newspaper editor Frederick Schley. Schley survived the attack and scathed that Johnson was a "desperate coward." Johnson's home was seized during the war by Union forces, forcing him to settle in Richmond, Virginia, after the war. (loc)

*   *   *

Throughout the fight, Lew Wallace remained at his headquarters. "The day was delightful," he recounted some fifty years later. "All under the cloudless sky lay in a shimmer of sunshine. The wheat fields, houses, barns, the visible church-spires—everything describable and indescribable entering into the composition of the scene lent it a homelike sweetness peculiarly attractive."

The bark of one of the 3-inch rifles sent to the front broke that a reprieve.

"Think I have had the best little battle of the war," Lew Wallace enthusiastically telegraphed back to Baltimore that evening. "Our men did not retreat, but held their own . . . . Losses unknown." One Federal aide would eventually hazard the guess

that "Our loss during the day was two men killed, one officer 17 men wounded; whilst the rebels reported loss was 140 killed and wounding"— though this sounds more like wishful thinking.

*   *   *

With the end of the fighting on July 7, Maj. Gen. Robert Ransom, commanding Early's cavalry, ordered his troopers back to the Catoctin. The withdrawal infuriated Bradley Johnson, who had asked repeatedly to push his advance into Frederick proper. Instead of continuing forward, Johnson dejectedly wrote that "we lay all day the eighth in a drizzling rain on the mountain."

Major General Wallace wanted more information about the force in front of him, though, and once more sent out David Clendenin. Captain Edward Leib and a small detachment of the 159th Ohio Mounted Infantry joined Clendenin's 8th Illinois, and together the horsemen set out. Again holding the vanguard, Maj. Harry Gilmor's Marylanders opened fire as the Federals "advanced boldly to the very base of the mountain."

The skirmishing continued throughout July 8, but did not reach the intensity of the previous day. "[The skirmishers went languidly on," Wallace later said. "Occasionally the artillery joined in and broke the monotony, the swish of the shells in flight giving the men lying upon the ground ... occupation, if not amusement."

Maj. Harry Gilmor commanded the cavalry's vanguard through Middletown. After the war, he served as both the police commissioner and mayor of Baltimore. (loc)

The "monotony" of the day would be broken, however, by the first arrival of Brig. Gen. James Ricketts's VI Corps veterans.

The voyage to the Monocacy had been absolutely exhausting: from the steamers in the Chesapeake Bay, the soldiers arrived in Baltimore late on July 7 and began to dock. From the ships, eager B&O Railroad agents ushered the soldiers onto waiting cattle cars, which started to slowly make their way out of the stations around 1:00 a.m. on July 8. Almost universally, the soldiers panned this ride. "The men passed a sleepless night on the crowded cars," one Pennsylvanian remembered. A New Jerseyan remarked that he and his comrades were "pretty tired of [the] U.S. transporting us around."

As the trains stopped at the Junction, Col. William Henry, commanding the 10th Vermont Infantry, climbed down to meet with Wallace. According to his orders, Henry was not even supposed to stop at Monocacy. While Henry's brigade commander, Col. William Truex, stayed at Baltimore to funnel more troops forward, Henry had gone ahead with the vanguard to keep the troops on the way to their original location, Point of Rocks, a point further down the B&O's tracks. But with Early's Confederates moving through South Mountain and onto Frederick, Wallace desperately needed help.

Wallace described the situation to Colonel Henry. The Vermonter already had an idea of what was going on, having guessed in a letter to his wife from the steamer on the way to Baltimore that Ricketts's division's goal was "to look after Genl Ewell [Early's predecessor]." Now Wallace filled in the rest, as up the road, Clendenin's troopers continued skirmishing. After the discussion, Wallace folded the new arrivals into his command, regardless of their original orders to continue to Point of Rocks.

Soon after, the fatigued soldiers clambered down from the cattle cars and began to brew badly needed coffee. After their voyage from Petersburg,

One of Frederick's most-noted inhabitants, Jacob Engelbrecht religiously kept a diary from 1818 until his death in 1878. On the afternoon of July 7, Engelbrecht climbed onto his roof to watch the skirmishing taking part on the western fringes of Frederick. (hsfc)

Col. William W. Henry of the 10th Vermont commanded the vanguard of James Ricketts's division. Continuing his service after the battle of Monocacy, Henry would be awarded the Medal of Honor for his actions at the battle of Cedar Creek in October 1864. (VThs)

Capt. Edward J. Leib's commission was with the 5th United States Cavalry, but along the Monocacy River he commanded the 159th Ohio Mounted Infantry, a new unit that needed the gaze of an experienced officer. In 1861, Leib had enlisted in the Washington Artillerists from Pottsville, Pennsylvania, one of the units awarded with a "First Defenders" medal because they had been among some of the first troops to reach a beleaguered Washington, D.C. (ht)

the Federals had empty haversacks and were thankful when Brig. Gen. Erastus Tyler's soldiers "generously shared . . . some of their own commissary supplies." The citizens of Frederick also pitched in with "some bread, meat, and coffee," something they continued to do as more of Ricketts's men arrived throughout the day. A later arrival from the 106th New York noted that "the people received us with joy giving water and provisions freely."

Henry's vanguard did not have much time to enjoy either coffee or food, though. Lieutenant George Davis, soon to be in the fight of his life, remembered "our coffee was nearly ready, when we were ordered to march to the east of the city." Wallace, it turned out, had some tricks up his sleeve as he waited for more of Ricketts's regiments to arrive. For the rest of the day he kept a handful of Federal regiments marching back and forth, kicking up dust and forming battle lines on hills and knolls, showing a force of strength and then double-quicking to a new location to give the impression of more soldiers. The Federal soldiers came to call one such rise "Deception Hill."

While Wallace put the vanguard troops to use in their deceptive marches, more arrivals came into the junction as the day went on, including men from Ricketts's second brigade, commanded temporarily by Col. Matthew McClennan. Ricketts and his entourage of staff officers, taking up the rear of the column, would not arrive until early the next morning, as even they fell victim to the laborious train ride. One of Ricketts's clerks remarked that they "Proceeded slowly, and after many delays, reached Monocacy Junction around 2 a.m."

But by the time Ricketts reached the Monocacy, the entire situation had changed.

Throughout the day, Wallace kept an eye on the mountains to his front, watching the dust trails kicked up by thousands of Confederates marching through the passes. Even with the steady arrival of Ricketts's men, Wallace would not be able to

As more of James Ricketts's soldiers arrived by rail, they clambered off their trains at the Monocacy Junction, seen here in 1858. None of these buildings still stand. (mnb)

fight Early on the northern side of the Monocacy River. No matter the odds, though, Wallace had already made a "determination to stand and fight." Washington, D.C., still lay undefended, and someone had to stand up to Jubal Early.

As evening came on July 8, Wallace began to bring his men back from the fringes of Frederick closer to the river. He had done everything he could do on the city-side of the river, and he had raised the alarm in Washington. At 8 p.m., he sent one final telegram. "Breckinridge, with strong column moving down Washington [Georgetown] Pike toward Urbana [a small town about five miles south of Monocacy Junction], is within 6 miles of that place," Wallace wired. "[I] will withdraw from Frederick and put myself in position to cover the road." As Wallace prepared to fall back across the Monocacy to take up battle positions, the telegram acted like an electric shock straight into Henry Halleck. He worriedly telegraphed Lieutenant General Grant, demanding more troops be sent from Petersburg for the defenses of Washington. But that would take time, and time had run out. Lew Wallace and his force of approximately 6,500 men would square off against Early's 15,000, and the result could determine the fate of the United States's capital.

The Battle's First Shots

CHAPTER SIX

JULY 9, 1864, EARLY MORNING

It rained heavily through the night of July 8, covering the Union retreat across the Monocacy. The Confederates, meanwhile, tried to stay dry up in the South Mountain passes. As the sun crested the horizon, though, the weather appeared to be shaping up for a perfect day. "It was a beautiful day in this beautiful country," a Confederate soldier remembered. "The sun was bright and hot, a nice breeze was blowing which kept us from being too warm, the air was laden with the perfume of flowers, the birds were singing in bush and tree[.]"A Federal soldier also noticed the birds singing, "which we had been so unaccustomed to hear during our late journey from the Rapidan to Petersburg[.]"

Wallace spread his forces across a front of about five miles, his battle line conforming to the contours of the Monocacy River. On his right flank, covering the Baltimore Pike and Stone Bridge, Wallace posted Erastus Tyler's brigade of Marylanders and Ohioans. Towards the center of his line, close to John Garrett's rebuilt iron railroad bridge and Monocacy Junction, Wallace held James Ricketts's division in readiness for whatever came down the road. Near the railroad bridge, Wallace also kept an eye on a wooden covered bridge that carried the Georgetown Pike across the river and straight

A cannon marking the location of a Confederate battery at the Best farm points menacingly across the Monocacy River. (cm)

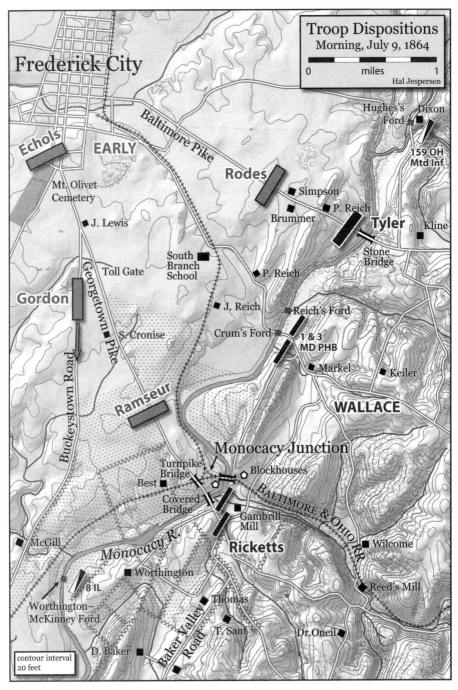

TROOP DISPOSITIONS, MORNING, JULY 9, 1864—Lew Wallace arrayed his outnumbered forces along the Monocacy River, defending the fords and bridges that Jubal Early would need to capture in order to continue his march on Washington, D.C. The fighting soon centered on two bridges near the Georgetown Pike and Baltimore & Ohio Railroad.

towards Washington, D.C. Above and below his main positions, Wallace posted Clendenin's cavalry to keep watch over the numerous fords that crossed the river.

To defend the Junction proper, almost three hundred men crossed the river and took up positions to act as skirmishers. About 200 of these men were led by Cpt. Charles Brown from the 1st Maryland Potomac Home Brigade. To supplement the Marylanders, 75 veterans from the 10th Vermont Infantry were detailed to help. Lieutenant George Davis, ordered to cross the river as well, remembered his orders were "to hold the iron bridge . . . at all hazards." The Vermonters—including privates Daniel B. Freeman and his skirmishing partner, George Douse (whose face would soon be injured)—took up position beside their Maryland comrades. Command of the whole force originally belonged to Lt. Col. Charles Chandler from the 10th Vermont, but he inexplicably, without telling anyone, re-crossed the river and spent the coming battle skulking in the Federal rear. When his absence was noticed, Captain Brown took command.

First Lt. George Davis found himself commanding the roughly 300 Union skirmishers on the far side of the Monocacy River away from the main Federal line. After Monocacy, he was wounded at both the battles of Third Winchester and Cedar Creek. Promoted to captain before the end of the war, he returned to Vermont and involved himself with numerous local Christian youth programs before his death in 1926. (mnb)

Near Frederick, Lt. Gen. Jubal Early's Confederates began to move out. Early did not join his forces that morning, instead taking up headquarters in Frederick where he dictated a letter to the town's leaders demanding $200,000. If the town did not pay, Early threatened, he would burn it. For the time being though, town officials refused to give in to Early's demands—what would be the purpose of paying if Wallace were to win the battle shaping up just three miles to the south? (The ransom of Frederick is discussed in Appendix B.)

All eyes turned anxiously to the river.

As the two sides closed in, some soldiers looked around and put the war on hold to admire the Maryland fields. One soldier wrote to his wife, "Kate, if I had a hundred acres of land near Frederick City, and paid for, I would never go back to York State again to live. Such a country is worth fighting for." A Confederate cavalryman shared the opinion, writing, "It is all together a most

The covered bridge over the Georgetown Pike needed to be defended at all costs by Federal forces if they were going to delay Jubal Early's Confederates. Already burned once before in 1862 by Confederates, the bridge had been rebuilt only to be put to the torch again, this time by Union soldiers, during the battle of Monocacy. (mnb)

Brig. Gen. Robert Johnston's North Carolinians led the way down the Georgetown Pike towards confrontation. Johnston served with Early throughout the Shenandoah Valley and, after the war, served as a lawyer and banker. He died in 1919 and is buried in Winchester, Virginia. (mnb)

magnificent and lovely country." That serenity, though, would soon be shattered.

Major General Stephen Ramseur led the way towards Wallace's force. Behind Ramseur's columns rolled numerous artillery batteries. Moving down the Georgetown Pike, one of Ramseur's brigades, commanded by Brig. Gen. Robert Johnston, fanned out into skirmish formation. Johnston's North Carolinians closed in on the Junction, but Captain Brown hesitated to give the order to fire— he thought "they were Union troops because [they were] dressed in blue clothing which they had recently captured at Martinsburg." George Davis "stoutly protested, telling him our friends were behind us," but still Brown gave no order. Then Johnston's men opened a sharp rifle fire, dropping a handful of Marylanders. After that, Davis explained that Brown "turned to me in disgust and insisted upon my taking command." Davis brought his Vermonters up, and Private Freeman later remembered, "We opened fire, and made them seek hiding places for protection, though they did not withdraw entirely." The two lines settled in and continued skirmishing.

Beyond skirmishing, Johnston's Confederates covered Lt. Col. William Nelson's artillery battalion as the gunners unlimbered. Among the first of Nelson's batteries to unlimber were Cpt. John Massie's Fluvanna Artillery and Cpt. Thomas Kirkpatrick's Amherst Artillery. Pushing a pair of 12-pounder Napoleons up to the Best farm, not far from Monocacy Junction, the

Confederates rammed shells home and then tugged on the lanyards. Fire and smoke bellowed from the cannon barrels as the thunderous shots of the battle's first artillery rounds screeched overhead.

Across the river, some of Ricketts's men were drawing rations when the shells landed. These Federals had clustered at Gambrill's Mill, next to a train recently arrived to deliver food to the men who had depended on handouts from Tyler's men. Massie's first shot struck these soldiers, leaving the bloody wreckage of two mortally wounded soldiers from the 151st New York. A soldier in the 126th Ohio later wrote, "it seems, Early sniffed our sow belly from a far, and wolf like, made a rush for it, but soon learned it would take some fight to get it." The Federals took up their rifles and prepared for action. In the ranks of the 151st New York, not far from where the first shell landed, Pvt. Philip Cook quickly jotted in his diary, "July 9th: Year 1864. The Battle of Monocacy is on."

In response to the Confederate guns, Cpt. Frederick Alexander's men jumped to their pieces. Alexander's battery of 3-inch rifles were scattered along the line and began to return fire. With more rebel pieces being brought into action, though, the Federal battery's historian recounted, "for every shot fired we received two in return."

Adding to the din was a 24-pounder howitzer, manned by a detachment from the 8th New York Heavy Artillery and located on the eastern side of the river, lobbing shells towards the deploying Confederates. Shortly before the shooting had started, Cpt. William H. Wiegel, an officer on Tyler's staff, had taken command of the howitzer's crew. Lew Wallace later remembered, "Wiegel's first shell burst above the gunners on the pike. Before . . . the white cloud left by the missile had disappeared . . . the pike was cleared."

Brigadier General Armistead Long, commanding Early's artillery, soon ordered more guns up to face off across the Monocacy. Captain

Thomas Kirkpatrick commanded the Amherst (Virginia) Artillery, who fired some of the first cannon shots of the battle. After his death a friend eulogized Kirkpatrick: "He was honest and true from boyhood to the end of his three score years, fearless in the maintenance of his convictions amongst his fellow men, and equally brave on the battlefield where the bursting shell and the hissing bullet told of danger and death." (cb)

Capt. Frederick Alexander commanded the Baltimore Light Artillery during the battle of Monocacy. His gunners, though badly outnumbered, kept to their pieces and safely brought all their rifles off the battlefield as the Union line collapsed around them at the end of the fight. (fw)

Daniel B. Freeman, profiled in the prologue, made this map detailing his actions at Monocacy (right). On the left of the map is "Freeman's Outpost," which would have been near the site seen in the modern photograph (above). (nt)(cm)

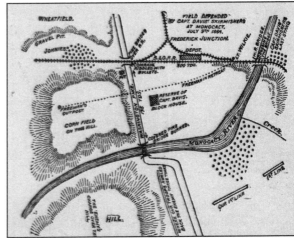

John Carpenter's Allegheny Artillery joined the firing line and opened fire not far from the Best house. The three batteries in front of Monocacy Junction now outnumbered Wallace's limited artillery, and Long still had an abundance of cannons in his reserve. With shells dropping all around, one exasperated Union soldier in the 110th Ohio wrote, "Oh if we had brought our [Army of the] Potomac battery with us then it would all have been right." The decision to leave behind the VI Corps's guns was coming back to haunt the Union forces.

With more of Ramseur's division deploying in the fields across from the beleaguered Federal skirmish line, three more companies from Ricketts's division dashed across the river to help out Lieutenant Davis and Captain Brown. These men came from the 9th New York Heavy Artillery, acting as infantrymen, and the 106th New York Infantry. Their added musketry bulked up the skirmish line, at least for the time being.

The battle of Monocacy was about two hours old, but little had been accomplished beyond making a lot of noise and smoke. Although little maneuvering had taken place, that would soon change, and the action would go from a loud skirmish to a full-fledged battle.

McCausland's First Attack

CHAPTER SEVEN

10:30 A.M.-12:30 P.M.

While the two sides grappled in their skirmish lines, the main question for Jubal Early's Confederates became how to get across the Monocacy River. Early's divisions could have formed strong battle lines and stormed forward, forcing the issue, but attacking across the river in the face of veteran infantry backed by artillery, limited as it was, would still have proven costly. Early later admitted this when he wrote, "The enemy's position was too strong, and the difficulties of crossing the Monocacy under fire too great, to attack the front without greater loss than I was willing to incur." This was the same reason Early had balked at attacking Maryland Heights—if his objective was threatening and capturing Washington, D.C., he could not throw his forces into an attack that would shred them and make them combat ineffective for the final push against the Federal capital.

Plenty of fords spanned the Monocacy River—the task for the Confederates was to find one relatively undefended and capable of getting troops into a position from which they could attack Wallace's smaller force. Brigadier General Bradley Johnson, the native of Frederick whose troopers had spent the last two days clashing with Federal cavalry, was the clear choice for such a mission, but

Staring through fence rails near the divide between the historic Thomas and Worthington farms, much as Federal soldiers would have done as John McCausland's dismounted Confederate soldiers came towards them. (cm)

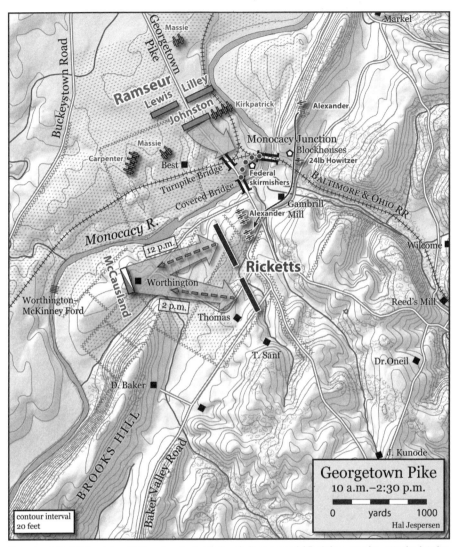

GEORGETOWN PIKE—John McCausland's brigade of dismounted Virginian cavalry attacked twice against James Ricketts's Union soldiers. At first, Ricketts only used one of his brigades but ultimately brought both of his brigades to bear as McCausland threatened to outflank him.

Johnson was no longer on the battlefield. On the morning of the 9th, Johnson's brigade set out on a mission personally conceived by Robert E. Lee: attack the Federal prisoner of war camp at Point Lookout, Maryland, and liberate the prisoners there, bringing them back to rejoin the Army of Northern Virginia. It was a wild goose chase that ultimately went nowhere (see Appendix D), but it took away the man most familiar with the

Brig. Gen. John McCausland (above) had originally commanded infantry during the war and, by the battle of Monocacy, only had about three months' experience as a cavalry commander. McCausland and his men went on to burn Chambersburg, Pennsylvania, (left) on July 30, 1864, in retaliation, they claimed, for David Hunter's treatment of the Shenandoah Valley. (loc)(loc)

ground when he was, arguably, most needed on the battlefield.

Jubal Early later claimed that he, personally, found a suitable ford to cross, but that's unlikely. Early remained in Frederick as his staff officers haggled with the town leaders over the ultimatum for $200,000, and it is not totally clear when he actually made it to the battlefield. One of his biographers guessed, "Only by 2:00 p.m. would [Early] personally view the ground," leaving battlefield dispositions until then to his second-in-command, John C. Breckinridge.

With Bradley Johnson's men unavailable to scout, the mission fell to the Virginians in Brig. Gen. "Tiger" John McCausland's cavalry brigade. Ranging to the south, about a mile and a half below the railroad junction, McCausland achieved his objective of finding a ford sometime around 10:30 a.m., according to one Federal staff officer's guess.

The ford lay in a curve of the river that brought a farm path across the Monocacy and up a hill to "Clifton," the home of John T. Worthington's family. Taking its name from the nearby home and another farmer's, the Worthington-McKinney Ford fulfilled the Confederacy's needs perfectly. McCausland's troopers began splashing across the Monocacy and climbing up the hill towards Clifton.

Wallace had not overlooked the Worthington-McKinney Ford, but his limited cavalry restricted how many men could watch the river crossing. Lieutenant George Corbit and his Company B, 8th Illinois Cavalry opened fire on McCausland's vanguard as the Virginians came across. Ordnance Sgt. James McChesney of the 14th Virginia remembered, "Genl. McCausland told us that he wanted us to cross as soon as possible," and the Virginians, using their numbers, quickly pushed Corbit's troopers back.

With their opposition out of the way, the Confederates moved across. "The Monocacy is a deep, sluggish stream with high slippery banks at the place which we crossed," Cpl. Alexander St. Clair, 16th Virginia, recalled. "We floundered through, filling our canteens with warm, muddy water which was to supply us through the burning hours of the day."

Looking down towards the Monocacy River. At the base of the hill, Lt. George Corbit's company of the 8th Illinois Cavalry briefly opposed McCausland's troopers and then retreated up the hill towards the camera. (rq)

Inside Clifton, the Worthington family sought cover from the battle heating up just outside—or at least they were supposed to be seeking cover. Curiosity got the better of six-year-old Glenn Worthington as McCausland's men came up to his home, and the little boy put his face up against the cracks of boarded-up windows, peering out as the troopers formed into a battle line. In 1932, Glenn, then a respected judge in Frederick, published *Fighting for Time: The Battle of Monocacy*, offering the battle's first full monograph. Worthington's book, recounting what he personally saw, remains a mainstay in Monocacy literature.

His family's ford proved especially useful for Confederate troops, Worthington wrote, because the troops, "were hidden from the view of the enemy by the thick foliage of the trees and bushes growing along the banks of the river." As soon as McCausland's troopers crested near Clifton, however, they were plainly discernible to the

Federals, including Lew Wallace. He quickly scribbled a message to James Ricketts. "A line of skirmishers is advancing from the south beyond the cornfield at your left," he recounted. "I suggest you change front in that direction, and advance to the cornfield fence, concealing your men behind it."

Ricketts heeded the message and soon had the bulk of his first brigade moving to counter the threat. His men ran to the fence line separating Worthington's property from that of C. K. Thomas, and ducked behind, planning to hide until the last moment. A cornfield, "about waist high," Glenn Worthington remembered, helped in the Federal concealment.

At Clifton, McCausland's men dismounted and readied to go forward. Traditionally when cavalry dismounted, every fourth man held the reins of his three other comrades, but John McCausland had other plans. Alexander St. Clair, with a fresh canteen of water, wrote, "when we reached the 'brick house' [Clifton] every man was ordered to dismount, tie his horse to the fence or turn him loose. No one could be spared to hold horses. We fully realized that this meant serious work, as this command had never before been given us."

In their battle line, McCausland's men set off down the hill and towards the Federal rear. With the Federals hiding behind the fence and corn, possibly the only Union soldier the Confederates could see was Ricketts himself, who remained "the only man on horseback. . . . His staff officers having dismounted," Glenn Worthington later wrote. The Confederates did not sense any opposition and moved "with banners and guidons waving and a general feeling of an easy victory prevailing." A soldier in the 87th Pennsylvania added that the Confederates "expected to meet raw troops," adding to their oblivious march forward. Ricketts waited for the perfect time to unleash his Federals.

That moment came when McCausland's men were "within 125 yards" of the Federal line. "Then, at a word of command, the whole Federal line of infantry rose to its feet and resting their guns on the

Glenn Worthington watched the battle of Monocacy from his family's basement. Six years old at the time, the memories of the battle stayed with Worthington for the rest of his life, and he was one of the strongest advocates for land being set aside as a permanent park to commemorate the battle. He was a successful judge in Frederick and is buried in Mount Olivet Cemetery. (mnb)

Col. William Truex, commanding a brigade in Ricketts's division, repulsed McCausland's first attack. Truex had attended West Point for two years, but left before graduating. He served in the Mexican War and joined the Union army as a major in the 5th New Jersey Infantry. Truex was new to brigade command at Monocacy—the result of heavy casualties in the Overland Campaign requiring replacement officers. (mcl)

upper rails of the fence, took aim and fired a volley, a murderous volley into the ranks of the approaching foe," Worthington remembered. "Watched from a distance the whole rebel line disappeared as if swallowed up in the earth. Save and except several riderless horses galloping about . . . the attacking force had vanished."

Corporal St. Clair wrote, "we were met by a withering fire from thousands of muskets. . . . We were ordered to lie down, as under this concentrated fire no living being could have stood."

As the Confederates began to return fire, thick, acrid clouds of dirty-white smoke formed in front of each line. Trying to get a better view of the Union battle line, Lt. Col. William C. Tavenner "called out for a volunteer to climb on his shoulders and from that elevation look down on the enemy's line," Nathan Harris, a trooper in the 16th Virginia, recalled. One of the lieutenants from the 16th offered, and Tavenner "bent down and the Lieutenant climbed on his shoulders, and then [Tavenner] slowly rose. He had scarcely straightened himself out," Harris wrote, "when there came a sharp sound from the direction of the enemy, and a volley was poured into the bodies of the two men. They fell to the ground and instantly expired, making no report."

McCausland's battered men began to retreat towards Clifton. "The officers tried in vain to rally the men," Glenn Worthington remembered. "They swore at them and threatened them with sword and pistol, but for a while they would give no heed." Tucked away inside the brick building, nonetheless, "The curses of the officers in their efforts to stop the men and their threats to kill the fugitives unless they turned could be plainly heard by the occupants of the cellar." Watching and listening, Glenn's mother, Mary, "was moved to exclaim: 'Poor creatures, it means death to them either way.'"

*   *   *

Around the same time that McCausland's advance was shattered, Stephen Ramseur attacked the Junction again. Ramseur ordered some of Robert Johnston's North Carolinians to once more go forward to try to push the Federals away from the Junction. Charging forward, the Tar Heels were soon hit "by a hot enfilading fire from the line of battle in the railroad cut," as one North Carolinian remembered. To escape the infantry and artillery fire, "a company of soldiers" from the 23rd North Carolina "passed under [a] culvert and opened fire on the Enemy in the R.R. cut from the left flank," one of Carolinians wrote. This flanking fire caused some of the Federal skirmishers to reel back, and one of the Confederate shots found George Douse (the unfortunate Vermonter) in the face.

Other Confederates sought a sharpshooting position in a barn on the Best farm. Climbing into the loft, the Confederates began to fire down into the Federal position and across the river. It was not long, though, until, according to the battery historian from the Baltimore Light Artillery, that "one of our officers noticed small puffs of smoke from under the shingles of a barn . . . we directed our attention to them, the second shot burst inside the barn, and so did the third, and the fourth; the barn was soon on fire." Scrambling for cover, the Confederates left the conflagration while, in Lt. George Davis's simple words, he "repelled the attack" on the Junction.

With the dull pop of musketry and occasional cannonading, the calm of earlier returned to the Junction.

* * *

While James Ricketts bloodied McCausland's cavalry brigade and Stephen Ramseur tried for the railroad junction, Maj. Gen. Robert Rodes's division also engaged on the north end of the battlefield, near the Stone Bridge and Baltimore Pike.

Rodes's men marched through Frederick around 11:00 a.m. before taking up their route on the macadamized Baltimore Pike. One Confederate officer, Cpt. Robert Park, harshly wrote that he "neither saw nor heard anything of

One of McCausland's troopers at Monocacy was Nathaniel E. Harris. Eighteen years old at the battle, Harris survived the war and went on to serve as governor of Georgia from 1915-1917. (nh)

Mary Worthington, Glenn's mother, was horrified watching the devastation of McCausland's brigade as they retreated from the Federals' fire. (mnb)

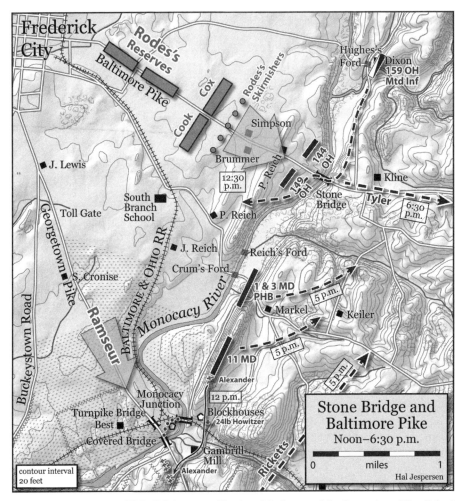

STONE BRIDGE FIGHTING—While fighting surged back and forth around the Georgetown Pike, Robert Rodes began to push against Erastus Tyler. The heaviest fighting for the bridge came around noon when Rodes attempted to capture the axis over the Monocacy River. After Tyler blunted the initial attack, the fighting near the stone bridge fell into long-range skirmishing until about 6:00 p.m., when the Union force began to fall back towards Baltimore. Tyler acted as the rearguard, fending off the last assaults.

the mythical 'Barbara Freitchie' [sic], concerning whom the abolitionist poet, Whittier, wrote in such an untruthful and silly strain." Barbara Fritchie, a resident of Frederick, had gained notoriety during the Antietam campaign in 1862 when, as Stonewall Jackson's troops marched through the town, she supposedly waved the Stars and Stripes in the Confederate faces. John Whittier, the "abolitionist poet," had written a popular poem describing the incident, which likely never happened. Regardless of whether Fritchie waved the flag, Captain Park would not have seen her in the summer of 1864— she had died in the winter of 1862, at the age of 96.

Rodes's orders did not call for a full-sized attack across the Monocacy. Rather, his division was to cover the left flank of Early's force and skirmish with whatever enemy it found to the front. With Early himself still in Frederick, Rodes was largely on his own.

Across the line, Brig. Gen. Erastus Tyler prepared his men. Tyler was responsible for protection of the Stone Bridge as well as a couple of fords across the river, including Hughes's Ford, to his north, and Crum's Ford, located almost at the middle point between the Stone Bridge and Monocacy Junction.

Using his tiny complement of horsemen, the 159th Ohio Mounted Infantry, Tyler screened Hughes's Ford. To protect Crum's Ford, Tyler looked to the remaining companies of the 1st Maryland Potomac Home Brigade—the others being under the command of Charles Brown at the Monocacy Junction—and the 3rd Maryland Potomac Home Brigade. To connect to the Junction from his line, Tyler positioned the 11th Maryland Infantry, the newest unit to have joined the service. That left Tyler with the two units of Ohio National Guard to face off against whatever Rodes sent his way.

Only three companies of the 144th Ohio had made it to the Monocacy, the others remaining behind to defend relay houses and other points along the B&O. With both the 144th and the 149th truncated, Tyler combined them under the command of Col. Allison Brown (not to be confused with Cpt. Charles Brown) and sent them across the bridge. The Ohioans took up positions in the fields, along the ridgeline in front of the bridge, and prepared to fight.

When Rodes came forward, he did not send his entire division towards the Ohioans' battle line. Rather, his division's sharpshooter battalions dashed ahead and began to take aim. The concept of

Barbara Fritchie, a native of Frederick, became a national icon with the publication of John Whittier's poem detailing her supposedly flying a United States flag in front of Stonewall Jackson's troops as they marched through town in 1862. The incident never occurred, though. Fritchie's neighbor, Jacob Engelbrecht, wrote, "I do not believe one word of it. I live directly opposite, and for three days I was nearly continually looking at the Rebel army passing the door... and should anything like that have occurred I am certain someone of our family would have noticed it. The first I heard of it was the Whittier poetry." Fritchie, who died in 1862 before the publication of the poem, is buried in Mount Olivet Cemetery. (loc) (cm)

The stone bridge brought the Baltimore Pike—or National Road as it is sometimes referred to—over the Monocacy River. As Wallace's only escape route back to Baltimore, holding the bridge was vital for the Union forces. The bridge no longer stands, but the "jug," seen on the eastern side of the bridge, still exists, and is included in the driving tour. From this photograph's perspective, Ohioans under Brig. Gen. Erastus Tyler were positioned on the far side of the river, skirmishing with Maj. Gen. Robert Rodes's men. (loc)

sharpshooter battalions had been introduced to the Army of Northern Virginia the spring before. Officers would pick the best shots among their units, and during battle, the chosen men would form into individual battalions. When the action was over, the men would return to their parent regiments until the next fight. While the rest of Rodes's division watched and waited, his sharpshooters went forward to engage Brown's Ohioans.

"Then came the tug of war," one soldier in the 149th Ohio wrote later. Allison Brown guessed that the enemy's sharpshooters hit his line around "11.30 a.m.," the same time as the escalation of the fighting around the Junction and Worthington Farm.

The sharpshooters soon held the upper hand. They spread out in a loose formation, making themselves harder to hit, while others went into a log house and began poking their rifles through "holes pierced in the chinking between the logs," one of Tyler's staff officers wrote. "So accurate was their fire that it was dangerous for our men to even show their heads above the hilltop."

Col. Philip Cook commanded one of Rodes's brigades of infantry. Rodes's division deployed its sharpshooters and did not really push the Federals until later in the day, leaving most of the Confederates there standing in reserve. (loc)

Other Confederates began to make their way around Colonel Brown's left flank, edging closer to the Stone Bridge. When the Confederates began to fire down Brown's line, he knew he had to do something. Turning to the 149th Ohio, he ordered a company to charge the rebel sharpshooters to push them back.

As the Ohioans set out, though, the Confederate fire hit them hard. "During this charge," Brown reported, "my loss was quite severe, owing to the fact that the enemy was posted behind the fence, while my men were compelled to charge across an open field, up the hill in fair view, and within short range of his guns."

As the Ohioans from the 149th reeled back, Brown sent more men in, this time from the 144th Ohio. Though they had only been in uniform for about three months, the companies from the 144th "never flinched but went at it like old veterans," an onlooker recalled. This time the Ohioans succeeded, and Rodes's sharpshooters fell back to where they could continue their long-range sniping with impunity. Colonel Brown solidified his line and waited for the next attack.

On both ends of the battlefield, the Confederate advances had been blunted. None of the attacks had been all that large, and a soldier in the 87th Pennsylvania remembered, "After the enemy had been driven back from the railroad, about noon, there came that ominous lull often spoken of before a storm."

That storm would soon come crashing down.

Col. Allison Brown oversaw both the 144th and 149th Ohio National Guard at Monocacy. He had enlisted as a private at the beginning of the war and steadily climbed through the ranks until he was commissioned as the colonel for the 149th Ohio in the spring of 1879. He served as a state senator in Ohio from 1875 until his death in 1879. His men affectionately called him "Colonel Ally." (gp)

McCausland's Second Attack

CHAPTER EIGHT

2:00-3:30 P.M.

Things started to go poorly for Lew Wallace as pressure mounted along his line.

First he lost the use of the 24-pounder howitzer that had been lobbing shells at Ramseur's skirmishers since the battle started. The gunners firing the howitzer were inexperienced and nervous, and as Confederates brought up more pieces of artillery, the situation became even more desperate. At some point, a jittery gunner improperly loaded the howitzer by ramming a shell home before the powder bag that was necessary to fire the artillery. In charge of the howitzer, Cpt. William Wiegel tried to unload the shell but was unable to do so. Getting word of the disabled howitzer, Wallace rode over to the vexed gun crew.

"Up-end the gun," Wallace ordered Wiegel, who replied, "I've tried that; it won't do."

Unable to get the shell out of the howitzer, the gun spent the rest of the battle lying dormant and useless to the Federals. "The howitzer alone was worth all [Frederick] Alexander's six rifles," Wallace remembered. The howitzer was "lost to us . . . when it could have done us infinite good."

Sometime between noon and 2:00 p.m., Wallace's next crisis reared its head. With Ramseur bringing more of his troops up to face off against the Federal line at the junction and John McCausland's

The modern bridge over Maryland Route 355 is located near where the covered bridge was before Federal soldiers put it to the torch. (cm)

cavalry brigade near the Worthington house, Wallace became increasingly worried about the wooden covered bridge. If the Confederates seized the bridge intact, it would serve as a dagger straight into the Federal lines, and Wallace did not have enough men to shuffle around to each point of contact. "My objective was to release the guard taking care of it [the bridge], and that they might join their regiments, then in ever such need of every available man," Wallace wrote later. Only one option remained: burn the bridge.

Blockhouses like the one seen in the middle of this drawing were constructed to defend key positions along the Monocacy River, such as the B&O Railroad bridge, seen in the background. The 24-pounder howitzer that was being used to such good effect before it was loaded incorrectly was positioned next to one such blockhouse. Retreating Federals burned the blockhouses, and their exact whereabouts today are unknown. (mnb)

Wallace's order passed down the ranks and came to the 9th New York Heavy Artillery. Soldiers "procured sheaves of wheat from a near-by field, and placed them under the southeast corner of the roof of the bridge," the New Yorkers' regimental historian wrote. Three soldiers went forward and lit the wheat; the fire soon "wrapped the roof in flames like magic." Glenn Worthington added more details, writing, "The dry shingled roof and long seasoned pine weather-boarding burned like tinder, and quickly the flames were mounting skyward. A great smoke began to fill the sky and blot out the sun. But the roaring flames did their work rapidly, and soon the large timbers began to fall into the water."

Before the bridge was burned, the New York companies skirmishing on the western bank of the river were withdrawn back across the Monocacy, but somehow the word to fall back did not reach either Lt. George Davis or Cpt. Charles Brown. Seeing his route across the Monocacy now a fully engulfed conflagration, Davis sent a man swimming across the Monocacy to try to get an explanation. The officer supposed to be in charge of the skirmish line (but who instead spent the battle hiding near the Gambrill Mill) sent back the baffling reply, "I supposed you was all over this side the river before the bridge was burned." Davis and Brown were on their own.

Wallace's shortage of troops to help defend all of his points could have been aided by more of Ricketts's soldiers, but in what became a third problem almost 1,000 of the division soldiers never showed up. Taking up the rear of the division's column, Col. John Staunton officially commanded Ricketts's 2nd Brigade. Staunton had two regiments of infantry and part of a third, but he spent the entirety of July 9 about eight miles from the battlefield. The soldiers with him never fired a shot at Monocacy, and a month after the battle, a court martial convened to try Staunton for his failure to appear on the battlefield. Brigadier General Ricketts testified that he had specifically ordered Staunton, on July 8, to move his men up towards the Monocacy Junction. For his defense, Staunton blamed B&O agents, one of whom, according to Staunton, had told him the railroad "had received orders to suffer no trains to pass beyond that point." Staunton also called a number of witnesses to testify that, throughout the day, they heard no cannonading to hint of a battle in the distance. The commission trying Staunton did not believe him, and it found him guilty of "Disobedience of Orders" and "Neglect of duty to the

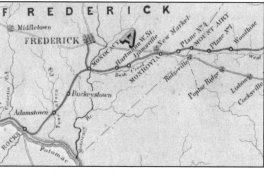

An inset of a map showing the route of the Baltimore & Ohio Railroad. While Lew Wallace's main force fought at the Monocacy, his only possible reinforcements—under Col. John Staunton—stayed eight miles away at Monrovia. (loc)

prejudice of good order and military discipline." Staunton was kicked out of the army and "forever disqualified from holding any office of honor, profit, or trust under the government of the United States." But Staunton's future punishment didn't help Wallace in the early afternoon of July 9.

Continuously looking for Staunton's men and never finding them, Wallace knew he could not hold off Early's forces indefinitely. Shortly after 1:00 p.m., Wallace sent a message to Ricketts alerting him to the situation and telling him to be ready to pull out when the Confederate pressure became too much. Ricketts passed along the message to Col. William Truex, holding the Federal line at the

Thomas farm, and added, "We are ordered to be ready at once to retire by the road to the Baltimore Pike." Wallace had admitted to himself that he would eventually have to retreat to Baltimore—the question that remained now was *when*.

*   *   *

"Tiger" McCausland caused another problem for Federal forces when he sent his brigade forward once again around 2:00 p.m. After their first bloody repulse earlier in the day, the Virginia troopers rallied near the Worthington farm. "It may appear almost incredible to one uninformed that soldiers who have just a few hours before been through a hell of deadly gunfire," Glenn Worthington wrote, "can be so soon rallied and again made to charge a foe superior in numbers . . . Yet that was the case done with these troopers [.]"

Instead of sending his men straight down into Ricketts's waiting men again, McCausland peeled his brigade off towards the right, hoping to outflank the Union battle line. Using natural folds of land, especially Brooks Hill next to Clifton, McCausland's men advanced towards Ricketts's left flank.

Taken from the perspective of the Federal battle line, this photograph looks uphill towards the Worthington farm. McCausland's men formed near the home and attacked downhill. Beside the Worthington house rises Brooks Hill. The bales of grain would have been scattered across the battlefield as the local families ceased their farming once the armies came into contact. Today, I-270 is located at about the middle of this photograph. (mnb)

The Union soldiers finally saw the Virginians as they came out from behind their natural cover and charged forward, yelling their rebel yells as they advanced. Outflanked, Truex's 1st Brigade started to fall back, yielding the fields around C. K. Thomas's farm to McCausland's men. Charging on the heels of the retreating Federals, the cavaliers took up position around the fort-like brick building and opened fire.

Reacting to the Confederate incursion, Colonel Truex ordered some of his regiments to mount a counterattack and push them out. To help extend the Federal line, the last of the reserves, the bulk of the 10th Vermont, was called to double-quick into position near the Georgetown Pike and Baker

Valley Road. With the Vermonters coming onto the scene, the majority of Truex's brigade attacked up the hill and into the face of McCausland's men.

Truex's men advanced "in gallant style," read the brigade's official report, "driving the enemy before them and occupying the [Thomas] house." The fighting was heavy and close, with the major of the 14th New Jersey writing that they engaged "the rebels around the corner behind the trees and everywhere else." One of Ricketts's staff officers wrote to his father that the Confederates retreated "with very heavy loss at the brick house especially on our left—when the road & yard were literally filled with them[.]"

Evicted from the grounds of the Thomas farm, McCausland's men retreated once again, moving back to the Worthington farm. The brigade's two attacks had cost it dearly in both enlisted men and officers, leaving a trail of dead and wounded that marked their furthest advances, but since McCausland never filed a report, getting an official tally is difficult. Alexander St. Clair remarked that "it seemed that the entire brigade would be killed or captured." But then, as the Virginians crested near the Worthington farm, their situation improved. "Soon," St. Clair wrote, "we were cheered by seeing Gordon's grey coats emerge from the woods on our right."

After having skirmished with the Federals at Harpers Ferry on July 6–7, Maj. Gen. John Gordon's division trailed the rest of the Confederate Army. On the morning of July 9, Gordon's men closed in on Frederick. "We marched leisurely along that morning in the direction of Frederick City," one of Gordon's soldiers, I. G. Bradwell, later remembered, "guying each other and feeling sure that our brigade of cavalry and our advance troops could easily drive out of our way any force of the enemy they might meet. But in this we were mistaken."

Gordon's men, for lack of a better word, lounged in the rear of the Confederate battle line. "We made ourselves comfortable and lay down under the shelter provided," a Confederate soldier wrote, "to *look* at the battle, something we had never done."

After McCausland's troopers gained possession of the Thomas farm, Federal soldiers organized a counter-attack. They pushed up from the base of the hill, charging towards the camera's perspective and pushing the Confederates out of the home and back towards their starting point at the Worthington farm. (rq)

The interior walls of the Thomas home still bear damage from the battle of Monocacy. The house today is park headquarters for the Monocacy National Battlefield and is open to the public only during specific events, so please check before entering. (rq)

But then, Gordon wrote, "About 2:30 p.m. . . . I was ordered by Major-General Breckinridge to cross the Monocacy about one mile below the bridge and ford on the Georgetown pike [sic], which was then held by the enemy." Grabbing their rifles and falling in, Gordon's three brigades made their way down to the Worthington-McKinney Ford to cross the river.

As his men waded the ford, Gordon "rode to the front in order to reconnoiter the enemy's position." He came across the remnants of McCausland's troopers and saw, in the distance, "the enemy was posted along the line of a fence on the crest of the ridge running obliquely to the left from the river." Seeing Ricketts's battle line in front of him, Gordon's task was finding a way to crack it.

John Gordon had some of the best troops in the entire Army of Northern Virginia to accomplish that objective. But that title of being the best had come at a devastating cost: his three brigades were a conglomerate, forced to consolidate in the wake of the bloodletting in the Overland Campaign. Combined, his three brigades had the remnants of 31 infantry regiments, but his division only numbered approximately 3,600. The division included the survivors of the famed Stonewall Brigade (the same brigade with which Thomas Jackson had earned his nickname, "Stonewall," at First Manassas), the ferocious Louisiana Tigers, and a brigade of determined Georgians that Gordon had commanded personally until recently. The Stonewall Brigade, consisting of five regiments, had been consolidated into a single regiment, yet still only numbered 249 men.

It was with this force of elite but depleted soldiers that Gordon now planned his attack.

Gordon placed his three brigades in a single line. On the right flank were Brig. Gen. Clement Evans's Georgians, the brigade that Gordon himself had commanded. Next to Evans, in the center, were the consolidated brigades of Louisianans under the command of Brig. Gen. Zebulon York, a son of Polish immigrants who had actually been born in Maine but who now fought for the Confederacy.

Brigadier General William Terry's Virginians, including the Stonewall Brigade and another brigade's worth of consolidated regiments, held Gordon's left flank.

Behind Gordon's line, Lt. Col. J. Floyd King, commanding a battalion of artillery, struggled to get guns into place to support the infantry attack. "On reaching the Monocacy it was found difficult to approach and even more difficult to cross with artillery," King reported. The artillerist finally managed to get one battery, the Monroe Virginia Artillery, over the Monocacy and up near the Worthington farm, where the gunners unlimbered. King decided to move his other batteries into enfilading positions on the western side of the river, where they could still do heavy damage to the Federal line without having to deal with the fords.

Once his three brigades and artillery support were in place, Gordon prepared to advance. He had decided to attack *en echelon*, meaning in a staggered wave formation, starting on the right with Evans's Georgians. The echelon formation was useful in order to isolate Federal units who would get sucked into defending against Evans's men, leaving York or Terry to advance a few minutes later and thus get into flanking positions.

It was close to 3:30 p.m. when Gordon started his attack. The climax to the battle of Monocacy was about to explode in a flurry of violence.

Bringing his division onto the field, Maj. Gen. John B. Gordon organized his attack in the same sequence that the brigade commanders are organized here (from left to right): William Terry, Zebulon York, and Clement Evans. They all commanded hard-fighting veterans, but all three men commanded little more than shadows of former brigades because of the heavy casualties earlier in the spring. (loc)(loc)(loc)

Gordon's Attack

CHAPTER NINE

3:30-5:00 P.M.

With his troops in place, Brig. Gen. Clement Evans was just about prepared to start Gordon's attack. Riding along the front of his line, Evans called out to his men, "We are now on the flank of the enemy. Their left rests on the edge of this wood in our front. You must advance quietly until you strike them, then give a yell and charge." One of McCausland's troopers also remembered that Evans arrogantly added, "Come on, Georgians, follow me—we will show these cavalrymen how to fight."

His speeches concluded, and with skirmishers leading the way, Evans gave the order to advance.

Calmly, Gordon watched them go. Observing Gordon's demeanor, one of his soldiers wrote, "I shall recollect him to my dying day . . . he was sitting on his horse as quietly as if nothing was going on, wearing his old red shirt, the sleeves pulled up a bit, the only indication that he was ready for the fight."

Evans's Georgians moved closer towards the Federal battle line holding steady near the Thomas farm. Near the left flank, the 10th Vermont's colonel called out, "Wait, boys, don't fire until you see the C. S. A on their waist belts and then give it to 'em." Then, as the Georgians reached the fence line dividing the Worthington and Thomas farms, the Federals curled their fingers around triggers.

"The command 'fire!' rang out along our line," a soldier in the 106th New York recalled, "then 'load

Looking from the 10th Vermont Monument over the ground where Gordon's men attacked. Dedicated in 1915, part of the plaque says, "This monument was erected by the state of Vermont to designate the position of the 10th Vermont Infantry during the battle fought here on the ninth day of July 1862 to save Washington, 'and we saved it.'" The Vermonters suffered 56 casualties during the battle. (cm)

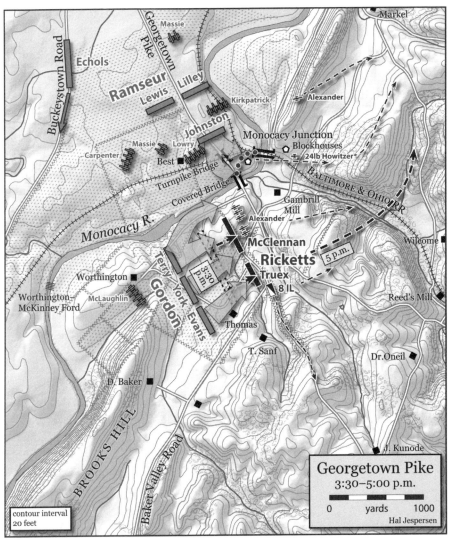

GEORGETOWN PIKE—Gordon's division of three brigades surged towards Ricketts's line and, in about an hour and a half, broke the Union line of resistance on Lew Wallace's left flank.

and fire at will,' and such a fire was kept us that no mortal power could face and cross that field."

John Gordon agreed with the New Yorker's assessment. "As we reached the first line of strong and high fencing," he wrote, "and my men began to climb over it, they were met by a tempest of bullets, and many of the brave fellows fell at the first volley." Georgians were shot down, leaving bloodied gaps where men had stood just moments before. The rest tried to push on.

Leading his men on horseback, Clement Evans soon became a casualty as a Federal bullet struck home. The worst damage to the brigadier general did not come from the bullet, though, but rather from Evans's pouch of sewing needles and clothing repair utensils. John Gordon remembered of Evans's wounding: "A Minié ball struck him in his left side, passing through a pocket of his coat, and carrying with it a number of pins, which were so deeply embedded that they were not all extracted for a number of years." Evans would survive his wound, but for now he was out of the action and command devolved to Col. Edmund Atkinson to continue the attack.

Pvt. George Nichols of the 61st Georgia charged forward towards the Federal line near the Thomas farm. (gn)

Evans did not have a monopoly on grizzly wounds. Private G. W. Nichols, fighting in the 61st Georgia, left a particularly gruesome memory. "Here I saw one of Company A of our regiment, Thomas Nichols (though no relative of mine) with his brains shot out. When I saw him he was sitting up and wiping his brains from his temple with his hand. I went to render him some assistance and did so by giving him some water. He seemed to have some mind, for he said he wanted to go back to Virginia and get a horse and try to get home and never cross the Potomac again. He lived twelve hours before death came to his relief."

In their uneven fight before the other brigades came up to help, the Georgians lost officers besides Evans as they tried to push against Ricketts. Colonel John Lamar, commanding the 61st Georgia, as well as his second-in-command, were both killed. Reflecting on Lamar's death, a Confederate officer wrote he "had but six months before married the charming Mrs. [Carter], of Orange county [sic], Virginia." The Georgians were being shredded, and they desperately needed help.

Gordon worked to bring up Zebulon York's Louisianans. The newcomers charged straight ahead, striking at Ricketts's troops around the Thomas farm. York reported that "My veterans marched under fire with the precision of automata." Closing in, the two sides continued volleying back

Maj. James Van Valkenburg took command of the 61st Georgia when its first commander, Col. John Lamar, was killed near the Thomas house. Leading the Georgians forward, Van Valkenburg was also killed. The two were buried on the Thomas farm the day after the battle in a small ceremony attended by John B. Gordon. Both men's remains were removed to Georgia after the war. Van Valkenburg had been heralded as the "hero of the Wilderness" when he had led an attack resulting in the capture of the 7th Pennsylvania Reserves on May 5, 1864. (Photo used with gracious permission by the Van Valkenburg Family Association.)

and forth, and York asserted that "Our fight at the Battle of <u>Monocacy</u> [emphasis in original] was of the [fiercest] and bloodiest that my command has ever been engaged in, considering the number ingaged [sic]."

The Confederates were making the Federals pay for their tenacious stand. Across the river and at the Worthington farm, Confederate gunners added their shells to the infantry's musketry. An officer in the 122nd Ohio, fighting on Ricketts's right, summarized the end result as "a murderous fire" that knocked men out of their ranks. To try to escape the bullets and shells, the Federals sought whatever cover they could, even utilizing the crop fields to their front. "[I]t is an interesting sight to see shocks of wheat used as a defense by our soldiers," the historian of the 9th New York Heavy Artillery remarked. "Also the hedges and trees in the Thomas yard are thoroughly utilized."

One of the New Yorkers wounded around this time was the regiment's colonel, William Seward, Jr., son of Lincoln's secretary of state. One shot brought down Seward's horse, and as the dying animal collapsed to the ground, it thrashed over Seward's leg and broke the bone. Two men helped get Seward and send him to the rear.

By now, the full force of Gordon's division pressed forward, and the division commander went in with his men, with a consequence. "In that vortex of fire," Gordon wrote, "my favorite battle-horse, presented to me by generous comrades, which had never hitherto been wounded, was struck by a Minié ball, and plunged and fell in the midst of my men, carrying me down with him." Unhorsed for a moment, one of Gordon's staff officers offered his own mount and the general climbed back into the saddle to continue the attack.

William Terry's Virginians advanced, moving to the left of York's Louisianans. The Virginians' adrenaline got the best of them, though, and they began to hustle, breaking their formations. "Stop running and walk," Terry called out to them, "or you will break yourselves down and we will not be able to fight the enemy when you get to them." Listening to their commander, the Virginians pulled up, readjusting their lines before moving on.

With pressure mounting, Ricketts's Federals began to fall back from the Thomas farm. From their first position, the soldiers retreated to the Georgetown Pike, which, because of years of use, had sunk down below the rest of the earth. This created a natural-made trench that the Union soldiers ducked into, hiding below the folds to reload and then peeking back up to fire.

Not all the Federal soldiers could fit in the pike itself, but they still found protection. The Georgetown Pike moved towards the Monocacy River and then swung to the east to reach the covered bridge, now just burning embers. But before the bridge's construction, the pike continued straight to the river to a ferry crossing. The ferry went out of business with the bridge's opening, but the sunken path down to the ferry still existed, and soldiers in Col. Matthew R. McClennan's brigade claimed that for their protection.

Ricketts's men had taken up position for their last stand.

Gordon's Confederates followed closely on their heels. Just as some of McCausland's men before them had taken up shelter in the Thomas farm, so now did Gordon's. Before they could do that, however, they needed to drive out the last stubborn vestiges of Federal resistance. A handful of Federal soldiers remained holed up in the Thomas home itself, firing out the windows as the Confederates closed in.

From the Worthington farm came the Confederate response: artillery. Guns near Clifton bombarded the brick Thomas home, and one of the shots "struck the side of the house at the dining room, crashed through the brick wall, fell on the table where a number of knives and forks lay, and exploding, scattered them in every direction." As Federal soldiers scrambled from the house, Confederate soldiers snatched them as a couple more shells hit the home for good measure.

The second son of Lincoln's secretary of state, William Seward, Jr., led the 9th New York Heavy Artillery into action at Monocacy. He recovered from his wounds at the battle and went on to a career as a banker, politician, and as an active member of the Military Order Loyal Legion of the United States, a fraternal organization for Union officers. (jwk)

Maj. Edward Dillingham of the 10th Vermont found himself caught up in the moment as he commanded infantry along the Baker Valley Road. "Give it to them, boys, we have on them on the flank," he called out, "pitch it into them; this is fun." The fun ended with Gordon's attack breaking through Ricketts's line. Dillingham was later killed at the battle of Third Winchester, in September 1864. (emh)

The Confederate sharpshooters, taking up places in the recently-evacuated home, began to fire down into the Georgetown Pike. Colonel William Henry, commanding the 10th Vermont, watched the sharpshooters' fire from the home until one of his soldiers "caught me by the coat-tail and pulled me to the ground, saying 'that will do, Colonel, the blooming rebs mean you.'"

Confederate artillery had cleared the Thomas farm, but it was not possible for Frederick Alexander's battery to do the same—they had run out of ammunition. The gunners had been engaged since first thing that morning and now, as watches clicked closer toward 4:00 p.m., there was nothing left in the ammunition caissons. It fell solely to Ricketts's men to fight against the Confederate onslaught.

But the Union infantry men were increasingly reaching into empty cartridge boxes, as well. After firing their last bullets, the soldiers took to "borrowing of their dead and wounded comrades," the chaplain of the 10th Vermont wrote.

Charging through the Thomas farm, Gordon's men closed on the Georgetown Pike. A small stream wandered across their front—not enough to pose an obstacle, but enough to leave a stark reminder of the brutal fighting. "In this ravine the fighting was desperate and at close quarters," Gordon wrote. "To and fro the battle swayed across the little stream, the dead and wounded from both sides mingling their blood in its waters; and when the struggle was ended a crimsoned current ran towards the river."

Federal and Confederate troops fired devastating volleys at close range, destroying ranks and leaving acrid smoke hanging thick in the air. "I recall no charge of the war, except that of [Spotsylvania's Bloody Angle] in which my brave fellows seemed so swayed by an enthusiasm which amounted almost to a martial delirium," Gordon remembered. Expressing a similar sentiment, a fighting man in the 126th Ohio jotted in his diary, "our brave boys like men battled with the tyrants with seemingly the energy of lions."

Watching his division's attack, John Gordon came to the conclusion that he needed help. "I dispatched two staff officers in succession to ask for a brigade to use upon the enemy's flank," Gordon reported. It did not take long for the officers to reach Gordon's superior, John C. Breckinridge, who had set himself up in the front yard of the Worthington farm. Breckinridge sent orders for his other force, commanded by Brig. Gen. John Echols, but Echols's division was still near Frederick, so it would be some time before they showed up.

In their stand-up, knock-down fight, it was not entirely clear just how much time Gordon's men had left in them; he couldn't wait. Riding over to William Terry, Gordon ordered the Virginians to move around Ricketts's right and outflank the Federals. The Georgians and Louisianans would remain where they were, holding Ricketts in place with their heavy musketry.

The Virginians started their move to the left. "This was the most exciting time I witnessed during the war," one of the Old Dominion soldiers wrote. Terry's men found a "hollow" that carried a small spring towards the Monocacy. "Concealed by the bank on their right these Confederate veterans reached the hollow almost unperceived," Glenn Worthington documented.

Union soldiers taking cover in the Thomas farm were soon sent scrambling for better cover when Confederate artillery opened fire on the house. Damage to the home's porch, no longer standing, was still visible in 1913. (mnb)

Though concealed from Ricketts's infantry, Terry's men were spotted by Confederate artillery crews across the river. Similar to how Ramseur's men wore captured Federal uniforms, it is likely that Terry's soldiers also exchanged uniforms when they captured Martinsburg, and as they advanced, the gunners across the river "mistook us for the enemy and fired at my flag, the balls striking very close," a Virginian recalled. Holding a Confederate battle flag, the soldier frantically waved his banner back and forth and as the wind

Virginians and Louisianans in Gordon's division were able to get extremely close to the Union battle line without being discovered by advancing behind the natural contours of the ground, which can be seen here. Popping over the hollows, the Confederates outflanked the Federals and began to push them back. (rq)

took hold of the Southern Cross, the Confederate batteries ceased firing.

Avoiding their close call with friendly fire, the Virginians pushed on until in a near-perfect flanking position. Popping out of the hollow, the Virginians began to fire into the ranks of Ricketts's right, held by troops in McClennan's brigade.

Simultaneously hit from the center by the rest of Gordon's men, the right by Terry's men, and the rear by Confederate artillery, McClennan's regiments started to break. The commanding officer of the 110th Ohio reported, "seeing the enemy coming down upon us in overwhelming numbers with imminent danger of having my command annihilated, I gave the order to fall back."

When McClennan's men started to fall back, Ricketts's entire line became unhinged. Confederate victory was close at hand.

The heaviest pressure of Gordon's flanking maneuver fell on Col. Matthew McClennan's brigade. McClennan held temporary command of the brigade in lieu of Col. John Staunton, its real commander, not being on the battlefield. (ol)

*   *   *

In conjunction with Gordon's attack, at 3:30 p.m., Stephen Ramseur unleashed a third attack on the Federal positions at the Monocacy Junction. His North Carolina skirmishers once more started to push forward, screaming the rebel yell as they went.

The North Carolinians had been stymied twice before, and the delay soured Brig. Gen. Robert Johnston, who, one of his subordinates recounted, "was not in a very humorous mood" as his men seemed unable to push the Federal skirmishers away. This time, though, the Confederates would not give up. "I was suffering (sick) so that I could barely walk," the 12th North Carolina's colonel wrote. "However, I went forward to the ravine [that had earlier helped the Confederates get close to the railroad junction] and here halted and had picked men as videttes to reconnoiter and see all they could." Their reconnaissance finished, the Carolinians surged forward.

Davis's and Brown's skirmishers held tenaciously for a little more than an hour. But then Charles Brown figured his men had had enough; earlier in the day General Tyler had given him "a discretionary order to fall back while I could do so with safety," and Brown decided that

moment had come. The Marylanders picked themselves up and ran across the railroad bridge ties, leaping from one track to another. On the other side of the Monocacy, Brown's men "occupied the rifle-pits" and continued firing.

Left behind on the western side of the river, George Davis needed to make a decision. His Vermonters, battered during the day and almost out of ammunition, were dangerously close to being cut off from the rest of Wallace's force. It was close to 5:00 p.m. now, and Davis later wrote that he looked to his left and saw "our third division line broken, scattered and fleeing." It was time to go—but the North Carolinians closed in quicker and quicker. "It was my last moment to escape, and in all human probability *too late* to escape."

But he had to try.

After being driven from their original line near the Thomas farm complex, Ricketts's men took up position in the sunken Georgetown Pike. Looking out over the fields in front of them, the Federals opened a devastating fire on the Confederates as they came over the hill in the distance. (rq)

The Federal Retreat

CHAPTER TEN

5:00 P.M.-MIDNIGHT, JULY 10

Lew Wallace had made his stand for as long as he could, but now it was time to go. Ricketts's division streamed from the Georgetown Pike towards the Gambrill Mill, near where Wallace had made his headquarters during the day. As the VI Corps troops retreated from Gordon's division, Wallace rode towards his right flank—Tyler's position at the Stone Bridge. With Ricketts used up, it fell to Tyler's Marylanders and Ohioans to cover Wallace's retreat to Baltimore, and he wanted to make sure they explicitly knew it. If Tyler retreated too soon and left the Stone Bridge open to Robert Rodes's division, Wallace's entire force could be encircled and destroyed.

Before riding to Tyler, Wallace watched Lt. George Davis lead his men to the railroad bridge. The iron trusses rose about 45 feet over the Monocacy River. What's more, the bridge had "no side rails for protection of pedestrians, and one in walking across, would have to walk on the cross ties, except that there was a narrow footway of boards through the middle." Because of the acrobatics needed to cross the bridge on foot, "it was against the rules of the [B&O] for any pedestrian to cross the bridge, except employees." But on this day, circumstances necessitated breaking the rules.

Charles Brown and his contingent of Marylanders had earlier managed to cross the

The monument to troops from Pennsylvania was dedicated in 1908, commemorating the actions of the 67th, 87th, and 138th Pennsylvania at Monocacy. Of those regiments, however, the 67th actually did not fight at the battle, instead waiting behind near Monrovia with Colonel John F. Staunton. (cm)

bridge with ease, but they were not being hounded by Ramseur's Confederates close on their heels. "[T]he enemy were probably not 20 feet behind us, calling out to surrender," Davis wrote later. Running with Davis, Pvt. Daniel Freeman remembered "one of my comrades under the Pike Bridge fighting a dozen Johnnies charging down the railroad toward him. He was riddled with lead."

The Vermonters pushed on, racing the Confederates to the other side of the bridge. At least one man lost his footing, Davis reported, and "fell through the bridge to the river . . . and was taken to Andersonville." Chasing their prey, the Confederates hurried on, led by the colonel of the 20th North Carolina, who "took the flag and lead the Regt across the R.R. Bridge in pursuit of the routed enemy."

Davis and his men made it across the bridge and hustled after the rest of Ricketts's division, the entire Federal force making its way to the Baltimore Pike. They managed to outrun their Confederate pursuers, who eventually grew tired of the chase and begrudgingly returned to the Junction. George Davis brought his men out from the clutches of the Confederates, and in 1892 received the Medal of Honor for his action at Monocacy. But it came at a cost for the 75 men who had gone out first thing that morning as skirmishers: Davis reported, "Of the 75 men . . . 15 were killed or wounded, and ten captured."

While Davis led his men to safety, another 10th Vermont soldier also distinguished himself enough to receive a Medal of Honor. Holding the left flank of Ricketts's division, the 10th Vermont did not hear the first calls to retreat from the Georgetown Pike. Riding up to

A dramatization of Lt. George Davis bringing his skirmishers over the Monocacy River by hopping over the railroad ties. (wfb/ofk)

the Green Mountain boys, a staff officer called out to the regiment's commander, "For God's sake, Colonel, get your regiment out of here as soon as possible to the Baltimore pike." Under a heavy fire from the Confederates seemingly closing in from every direction, the Vermonters retreated as quickly as they could. In the middle of the retreat, Cpl. Alexander Scott took one of the regiment's flags and began to carry it to safety when the other of the regiment's color bearers pleaded with Scott to also take the second flag, too exhausted to carry it further. Now carrying the Stars and Stripes as well as the regimental flag, Scott "carried both stands of colors through the trying ordeal of retreat and did not give them up until he returned them to their appointed custodians several days later," the regiment's historian wrote subsequently. Scott's bravery was recognized with a Medal of Honor in 1897.

Nineteen years old at the battle of Monocacy, Alexander Scott immigrated to the United States with his family from Canada as a young boy. When the Civil War started, his father enlisted in the famed Vermont Brigade and died of sickness in 1862. Scott enlisted shortly before and, because of his actions in the fall of 1863, was promoted to corporal. Wounded at the battle of Cedar Creek in October 1864, Scott earned a medical discharge, lived the rest of his life in Vermont, and is buried in Arlington National Cemetery. (mnb)

Beyond Davis and Scott, the rest of Ricketts's division had dramatic escape tales. Some of the regiments began to break down, and the retreat became an every-man-for-himself scramble. "I got separated from the rest," a soldier in the 151st New York wrote to his wife. "I put for the woods and laid down to rest a little, and the first thing I knew the 'rebs' were all around the woods and I couldn't get out. It wasn't long before some of our men came where I was in the same fix I was in, so we kept ourselves hidden." The New Yorker and his comrades were not discovered.

The adjutant of the 8th Illinois Cavalry had an especially hair-raising adventure. He got in a race with a mounted Confederate with a fence separating the two. As they rode, the adjutant "turned and fired a shot, as he said, for his mother. After exhausting his charges, he threw his pistol at the rebel." The Illinoisan was captured, but later escaped.

Then there were those Federals who were captured and did not manage to get away. Retreating towards the Baltimore Pike, Pvt. Alfred Roe of the 9th New York Heavy Artillery was stopped by a cry of, "Look here, Yank!" Turning, Roe "found myself gazing into the mouth of a six-shooter, held in the

Alfred S. Roe fought with the 9th New York Heavy Artillery at Monocacy. Captured in the confusion of the retreat, Roe was rounded up with the rest of the prisoners and eventually brought to Danville, Virginia. At the end of almost eight months in captivity, the exchanged Union soldiers "reaching the Federal lines, barely had strength to greet their friends," Roe wrote. (ar)

hand of a stalwart cavalryman." The Confederate demanded Roe empty his pockets, only found 35 cents and asked angrily, "Is that all you have?" When Roe told him yes, the cavalryman spat, "Well, keep it then. It isn't worth taking." Roe and the other prisoners of war were rounded up and brought back to the Georgetown Pike.

*   *   *

Those Federals who made it to the Baltimore Pike were covered by Tyler's brigade, still standing in their battle line. Covering Wallace's retreat, Tyler's men had one last action to fight out at Monocacy. Near 6:00 p.m., Rodes, who had been content with skirmishing the entire day, once more ordered his troops forward to force the crossing at the Stone Bridge.

Two of Rodes's brigades, commanded by Col. Philip Cook and Brig. Gen. William Cox, advanced on Tyler's Federals. Standing with his combined 144th and 149th Ohio, Col. Allison Brown reported that the Confederates attacked "along my entire front, and at the same time my left flank was turned. I now discovered that the enemy had gained a position in the woods, on the east side of the river in my rear, and was preparing to take possession of the bridge, thus cutting off my retreat entirely."

Brown's men fired into the oncoming Confederates, but Rodes's men, as well as some of Ramseur's, soon started to have the advantage. Firing back into the Ohio ranks, the Confederates bowled many of the Federals over. Colonel Brown, in the midst of the heavy fire, gave the order to retreat. "Our men are getting cut all to pieces. Every man must save himself," an Ohio musician in the rear worriedly wrote in his diary.

As Tyler's brigade broke to cross the Stone Bridge back to the east side of the Monocacy, some of the Ohioans "continued firing as they ran until the Rebels got so close to them that they had to throw away their guns to escape." Tyler's men made it to their bridge, but as at the railroad bridge, the Confederates pressed close on their heels. "I will not pretend to give you a faint idea of the terrible sight which was presented to the beholder," an Ohioan wrote.

On the eastern side of the Monocacy, Colonel Brown managed to rally some of his men in an orchard, and they "fired several rounds at the enemy. . . . This checked the pursuit, and enabled the main part of the command to gain the road on the hill." After Brown's quick rally, the Ohioans took up a quick step on the Baltimore Pike and retreated from the field. Going into the fight with some 600 men, Brown was only able to get about half out of the position, a testament to the confused and chaotic conditions around the Stone Bridge.

General Erastus Tyler nearly became a casualty as he tried to get his brigade off the battlefield. Riding down the Baltimore Pike, the Federal officers "came upon a squad of rebel cavalry," one of Tyler's aides wrote. "Seeing that we were Federal soldiers they fired upon us, and either wounded or captured our Orderlies. We at once put spurs to our horses and dashed down the road for about a mile, when, discovering that they were pursuing, and as our horses were well worn out, would soon overtake us, we turned from the road into the woods[.]" The maneuver allowed Tyler and his staff to lose the Confederates, but they spent the next two days hiding in the woods until found by Federal cavalry.

*   *   *

The last fighting on July 9 between the two sides came about five miles south of the Monocacy

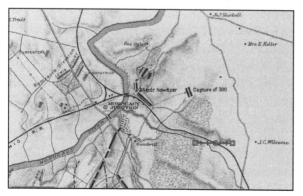

Of the 600 Union soldiers captured during the battle of Monocacy, half of them were scooped up during the retreat away from the Georgetown Pike and towards the Baltimore Pike, as is evident in this inset from a map drawn by Jedediah Hotchkiss. (loc)

Left to cover the retreat, Erastus Tyler's men fell back from the stone bridge and tried to hold for as long as possible. The Ohioans and Marylanders with Tyler fought until they "learned that the main body of our army had moved away an hour and a half or two hours before," a staff officer wrote. (lw)

Junction. Whereas the rest of Wallace's force retreated towards the Baltimore Pike, the 8th Illinois Cavalry had made its way south on the Georgetown Pike. Pursuing them were the tired and bloodied men in John McCausland's Virginia brigade. The two sides sparred along the Georgetown Pike until the 8th Illinois arrived at the small town of Urbana.

Leading McCausland's brigade, the 17th Virginia closed on the Illinoisans. Turning to face the Virginians, the 8th Illinois opened fire with their carbines and charged into the Virginians' midst. In the middle of the cavalry melee, the bearer of the 17th's flag was shot and dropped the flag. Scooping up the prize, the Illinoisans separated and repulsed a second attack that the Virginians made, killing the 17th's major in that repulse. Breaking off from the engagement, the 17th returned to the Monocacy River, having added to their butcher's bill from earlier with Ricketts. David Clendenin gave the captured flag to Lew Wallace, who later hung the flag in his hallway, and wrote that "the light breaking over my shoulders has a trick of turning the starred symbol into a red flash of such electrical effect that I must stop and look at it."

As the Federals retreated from the battlefield, leaving the Confederates as the unquestionable victor, the town elders of Frederick had no choice but to acquiesce to Early's ransom for $200,000. The money was split between the town's banks, and the citizens of Frederick gradually paid back the money over nearly 100 years, paying the last remainder in 1951.

Jubal Early's pursuit of Wallace's defeated forces only lasted a couple of miles before he called it off. In his memoirs, Early said he decided to stop because he "did not want prisoners" that would inevitably slow his column. Regardless of whether he wanted them or not, during the battle and its aftermath, Early's men captured about 600 men.

Beyond the captured, Early also inherited a bloody battlefield that he needed to tend to. The daylong fight along the Monocacy had led to approximately 2,100 casualties: 1,200 Federal and 900 Confederate. Subtracting the prisoners of war, there were 600 wounded and dead Union soldiers who lay across the field, stretching from the Baltimore Pike to the Worthington and Thomas farms. The heaviest concentration of Federal casualties fell at the Thomas farm, where Ricketts's division suffered close to 1,000 losses, as opposed to Tyler's brigade, which lost about 200 men at the Stone Bridge.

The wild cavalry melee between the 8th Illinois Cavalry and the 17th Virginia Cavalry outside of Urbana closed the fighting on July 9. Having already lost their colonel attacking near the Thomas farm, the Virginians lost their major as well as their flag to the Illinoisans. (lw)

Similarly for the Confederates, the heaviest losses came on the Southern end of the battlefield. Though records aren't clear, it's likely McCausland's brigade suffered about 150 casualties in both of its attacks. Gordon's division, by far, had the heaviest Confederate casualties of the battle. Advancing into battle with about 3,500 men in his three brigades, by the end of the fight Gordon lost 419 men in Evans's brigade, 116 in Terry's, and 163 in York's, for a total of 698—approximately 20% losses.

In comparison to the fight at the Thomas farm, Confederate casualties elsewhere were extremely light. One historian guesses Rodes's sharpshooters had 20 men killed or wounded at the Stone Bridge, and Ramseur probably lost a similar number since the 20th North Carolina, the regiment in his division with the most losses, came away from the Battle of Monocacy with 11 total casualties. John

Nicknamed the Nighthawk Rangers, the 17th Virginia Cavalry lost their flag at Urbana. Presented to Lew Wallace, the flag hung above his study in Indianapolis for years. It is now preserved in an enclosed case at the Monocacy Battlefield Visitor Center. (cm)

Echols's division had spent the entire day in reserve, and though Breckinridge called it up later in the day, it did not fight and thus did not suffer any casualties.

The Confederate troops tended to the battlefield, trying to care for the wounded when they could and settling down after the day's fight. One of William Terry's men found a full haversack on a dead Union soldier and that night he "ate a good supper out of my Yankee haversack and soon went to bed for the night." Others, though, had their sleep interrupted. One of McCausland's troopers bivouacked near "a small ravine near the center of the hardest fighting and down this ravine a stream was running." Throughout the night, the trooper wrote, "A number of the enemy's wounded had rolled down the banks into the stream. I could hear them turning in the mud and water, like hogs in a wallow, all through the night." The care of the wounded continued into the morning and beyond (see Appendix C for full details).

When looking at the battle of Monocacy, its casualties do not amount to an Antietam, Gettysburg, or Chickamauga, but Lew Wallace's stand nonetheless had crucial ramifications. He had gone to the Monocacy River to defend the B&O Railroad bridge and delay Jubal Early's Confederates. Wallace failed to defend the bridge, but he *did* delay Early.

But had he delayed Early for long enough?

*   *   *

About the time that Colonel Brown covered Wallace's retreat, Lt. Gen. Ulysses S. Grant telegraphed George Meade: "Send in the balance of the Sixth Corps to be forwarded to Washington." Though it took about two hours for Meade to get Grant's directive, he quickly replied, "The Sixth Corps has been ordered and will proceed at once to City Point." Just as Ricketts's division had marched

The end of the fighting left a battlefield scattered with carnage. Dead and wounded lay in contorted forms, and it fell to the Confederates to clean up the field. Reflecting on the heavy losses of his division in the fighting, John B. Gordon wrote two days later, "Oh Lord why am I spared & so many & so good men are taken around me. I cannot repay such mercy." (nyin)

to the steamers three days before, now the rest of the corps began to stir.

Marching out at 9 p.m., the Union soldiers made good time. Their march to the steamers, though, was much easier than Ricketts's dry, dust-choked maneuver, with the Sixth marching quickly in the middle of the night without the restrictive heat. One of Meade's staff officers jotted in his diary, "The remainder of the VI Corps left for Washington, at 11 this night."

Help was on its way to the Union capital.

Fort Stevens

CHAPTER ELEVEN

JULY 10-14

The Confederates set off early on July 10, with John McCausland's cavalry brigade taking up the vanguard. Following the Virginia cavalrymen, John Echols's division, which hadn't fired a single shot the day before, took up the march.

While Early's advance set out, some of his other men targeted the iron B&O bridge. One of the Confederate soldiers trying to bring down the bridge wrote, "We also burnt and destroyed the Government Horses Depot and etc. tearing up the B&O RR and battering down the magnificent iron bridge with artillery." Early's men did substantial damage to the junction, but they did not fully destroy the bridge, as evidenced by the railroad company's own annual report, where they reported the bridge "much damaged by cannon shot." Days after the Confederates had moved on from the junction, railroad workers made their way to the Monocacy and repaired the bridge, putting it back into service by July 17.

The last of Early's men moved down the Georgetown Pike around 1:00 p.m., the whole column snaking its way towards Washington, D.C. Morale remained high after their success the day before against Wallace. "This is the first victory we have gained north of the Potomac," wrote one soldier in Terry's brigade, "but I hope it may prove the precursor of many others."

The Secretary of the Navy Gideon Welles (left) thought little of the response from Secretary of War Edwin Stanton (right) to the news of incoming Confederates. (loc)(loc)

That morale and hope began to break down, though, as the Confederates ran into a new foe—the weather. By 2:00 p.m., the temperature reached a stifling 92 degrees; at 8 p.m. the heat had only dropped to 82. One after another, Confederate accounts seem to unanimously mention the heat and the chaos it caused on the Confederate columns. "The day was very warm and dusty," cartographer Jedediah Hotchkiss wrote simply, but another soldier explained what the heat truly caused when, in his next day's journal, he wrote, "I broke completely down yesterday. I have heretofore bragged of my endurance in marching; and for the first time in my life am too foot-sore to talk any further." Early's men marched about 20 miles on July 10 before stopping to sleep. The next day, Early figured, would bring his troops to Washington's front door.

*   *   *

Fear and uncertainty gripped Washington, D.C. With the VI Corps still making its way from Petersburg and the city's best garrison troops long-since stripped away for Grant's use in Virginia, Federal officials now scrambled to patch together a defensive force to protect the capital. "The alarm in that city was intense," an artillery officer remembered.

The military's response did not impress some of Lincoln's cabinet members. Attorney General Edward Bates wrote in his diary that he thought the Union generals, even Wallace and Sigel, "are helpless imbiciles." Secretary of the Navy Gideon Welles struck hard, noting, "It is evident there have not been sufficient preparations, but they are beginning to move. Yet they hardly have any accurate information." Welles derided that Secretary of War Edwin Stanton "seems stupid, Halleck always does." Welles continued on to make an extremely pertinent observation: "I am not, I believe, an alarmist, and, as I have more than once said, I do not deem this raid formidable if rightly and promptly met, but it may, from inattention and neglect, become so. It is a scheme of Lee's strategy, but where is Grant's?"

Grant and Halleck, after shrugging off Early's invasion for so long, now had to play catchup. Halleck, especially, had to eat his words. On July 5, he had wired Grant to say, "Although most of our forces are not of a character suitable for the field (invalids and militia), yet I have no apprehensions at present about the safety of Washington, Baltimore, Harper's Ferry, or Cumberland." Now, though, five days later, Halleck had to rely on those same "invalids and militia," and there certainly was apprehension about Washington's capture.

A mixture of forts, redoubts, and other earthwork positions surrounded Washington, D.C. In 1862, a commission of engineers working on the forts had filed a report that suggested, "The total infantry garrisons required for their defense . . . is about 25,000." The commission added that to operate the hundreds of cannons emplaced around the city would necessitate "about 9,000." Of those 34,000 troops that the commission had recommended, the Federal authorities could rely on a little more than 14,000 "present for duty," but of this number, most were convalescent or light-duty troops not suited to go toe to toe with Early's men.

To respond to the threat while waiting for the veteran troops of the Army of Potomac, Federal authorities looked to every source. Montgomery

The reconstructed Fort Stevens was put together in the 1930s by the Civilian Conservation Corps (CCC), a New Deal program during the midst of the Great Depression. A 2009 National Park Service (NPS) report on the status of preservation at Fort Stevens wrote, "Only those portions of the battlefield owned by the NPS retain integrity. All other areas have been altered beyond recognition since the period of significance [1864] due to intense growth of the surrounding metropolitan area." Thus, the work by the CCC remains vital to interpreting the events of July 11-12, 1864. (rq)

Before reinforcements arrived in Washington, D.C., civilian clerks like these men were called to arms. Woefully ill trained, they nonetheless faithfully manned the defensive works around the city, holding long enough for the VI and XIX Corps to arrive. One civilian employee, E.S. Bavett, was killed and another wounded. (fm)

Meigs, quartermaster of the army, even called out his clerks and office managers. The office men had some formal drilling, but that had been, in Meigs's words, "over a year since, but the arms then issued having been recalled, the organization in the departments of Washington and Alexandria had not been kept up." Holding muskets for the first time in more than a year, the clerks first needed refreshers on loading, firing, and maneuvering on the battlefield before they could go into battle.

In the midst of this emergency, Halleck became inundated with telegrams from those offering their assistance to command—not to fight, but to command—and Halleck finally snapped at one man in New York City, "We have five times as many generals here as we want, but are greatly in need of privates. Any one volunteering in that capacity will be thankfully received."

And so July 10 passed, with Jubal Early's force, dogged by the heat, marching towards Washington, and the Federals scrambling to meet them.

*   *   *

On July 11, Robert Rodes's division took up the vanguard for the rest of the march into Washington. The heat continued to be a problem, with more men falling by the wayside, but by noontime, the Confederate infantry pulled up near Silver Spring, the mansion belonging to Francis Blair, the father of Lincoln's Postmaster General, Montgomery Blair. From Silver Spring, the Confederates were four miles from the Capitol building. Captain Robert Park, 12th Alabama, noted that his men "are full of surmises as to our next course of action, and all are eager to enter the city."

Early's other divisions came up behind

The defensive bastion where Early's invasion ground to a halt was originally constructed as Fort Massachusetts in 1861 (left), manned by men from the 3rd Massachusetts Heavy Artillery. After the death of Isaac Stevens (above), at the battle of Chantilly on September 1, 1862, the fort got a new name. (loc)(loc)

Rodes, and as the soldiers glanced Washington in the distance, "The sights of its domes and fortifications fired anew my men," Brig. Gen. Zebulon York wrote.

Before getting to the Capitol, though, the Confederates had to get through the ring of defenses about two miles away.

Seeing the Confederates advancing about two miles from their position, Union artillery opened fire. The heavy guns, some firing projectiles weighing 100 pounds, soared through the air and exploded as Rodes deployed the same sharpshooters that had fought at Monocacy two days earlier. One Confederate soldier yelled out that "the cursed Yankees are throwing flour barrels at us," but the artillery fire, at that range and with the inexperienced gunners manning them, proved more a nuisance than a real threat. Exploding behind them, one Confederate soldier dismissed the artillery, writing, "we have never seen artillery used with such poor effect."

Rodes's sharpshooters advanced towards the fortifications, and they soon ran into the emergency forces that Halleck and others had thrown into the mix to cause delay. The inexperienced Union soldiers gave ground steadily, falling back to their forts. Following the sharpshooters, Rodes's entire division excitedly advanced.

But then, suddenly, orders came to stop. In the

Brig. Gen. Frank Wheaton's men landed at the Sixth Street Wharf and double-quicked to Fort Stevens. After the Civil War, Wheaton served in the regular army and fought out west. He died in 1903 and is buried at Arlington National Cemetery. (loc)

distance, beyond the fortifications, Jubal Early saw clouds of dust rising, kicked-up by thousands of marching feet. The VI Corps had arrived.

* * *

Lincoln personally waited at the Sixth Street wharves, watching the steamers getting closer and closer. The ships docked at noontime and soon began to offload their complement of troops. As the planks were lowered and the veteran troops in Maj. Gen. Horatio G. Wright's corps disembarked, they were met by more than their president. Throngs of people gathered to greet them, some cheering, others pleading for help. "The people in Washington seemed to be very happy to see us and were much frightened," one of the Federal soldiers wrote.

But as more of the soldiers offloaded, the citizens began to relax. "We had never before realized the hold which our corps had upon the affection of the people," a soldier remembered. "Washington, an hour before was in a panic; now as the people saw the veterans wearing the badge of the Greek cross [the VI Corps insignia] marching through their streets, the excitement subsided and confidence prevailed."

Wright's men made their way through Washington, at first unsure which way to march before some staff officers pointed them towards Seventh Street. Filing through the city, the soldiers came to Fort Stevens, the main bastion defending Seventh Street (today Georgia Ave). Originally built in 1861 as Fort Massachusetts, the fort had since been added onto, and renamed in 1862 for Brig. Gen. Isaac Stevens, killed at the battle of Chantilly. Now Fort Stevens would host the last battle of Early's invasion.

Since their halt, the Confederate troops had remained in place, sharpshooting and ducking from incoming Federal artillery rounds. Having realized that Federal reinforcements were arriving, Early balked at ordering an attack on the fortifications. "Under the circumstances, to have rushed my men blindly against the fortifications, without understanding the state of things, would have been worse than folly," he wrote later.

When the VI Corps troops arrived at Fort Stevens, their first objective was to clear the Confederate skirmish line away from the front of the fort. A brigade of troops, under the command of Brig. Gen. Frank Wheaton deployed in front of the fort, and a heavy skirmish broke out. Gradually Wheaton's men pushed back the Confederates, the two sides firing into the growing darkness. Early pulled his men back towards Silver Spring, then "held a consultation" with Breckinridge, Gordon, Ramseur, and Rodes.

According to one witness, Early's infamous temper appeared during the meeting with his commanders, blaming them: "You have ruined our whole campaign . . . [I]f you had pushed in the Forts this morning . . . we could have taken them—Now they have reinforcements from Grant & we can't take them without immense loss perhaps tis impossible."

The largest prohibitor to Confederate success on July 11, however, was not any one commander's decision but rather the extreme heat. With thousands of men falling out of line, many of the regiments could

not have mustered many men in the ranks even if Early had ordered an all-out attack on the capital's defenses.

Early and his commanders decided to wait for morning and try the works one more time, but during the interlude, Early received a message from Bradley Johnson, returning to the army from his failed raid (see Appendix D). Johnson warned Early that additional reinforcements, these from the XIX

The fighting at Fort Stevens resulted in more skirmishing as opposed to full-scale attacks. Both opposing armies were experts at such fighting by the summer of 1864. Thus, rather than resulting in heavy casualties, the fighting at Fort Stevens resulted in surprisingly light losses for both forces. (fl)

Before retreating into Virginia, Confederates burned the home of Lincoln's postmaster general, Montgomery Blair (above). All that was left of the home were some of the exterior walls, which were barely standing on their own when photographed. (loc)(loc)

Corps, would soon arrive and shore up Washington's defenses even more. The new intelligence "caused me to delay the attack until I could examine the works again," Early wrote later.

With daylight on July 12, Early rode forward and "found the parapets lined with troops." A last dash against the works was out of the question. And, now that daylight lit the battlefield, Early needed to delay until darkness would cover his retreat back to the Potomac River.

As it had the day before, sharpshooting and cannonading characterized the fighting outside Fort Stevens on July 12. Some of the Confederate soldiers, unaware of Early's decision to not attack, still waited for the order. "We looked every minute for the battle to begin, but with the exception of heavy skirmishing and some artillery firing on the Georgetown Road, there was none," a soldier in Ramseur's division wrote.

Inside Washington, much of the fear had dissipated with the arrival of the VI the day before. President Lincoln, noted one of his secretaries, "seemed in a pleasant and confident humor today." After his morning business Lincoln went about his day, but the sound of the skirmishing and cannonading proved too tempting. In the afternoon Lincoln got in a carriage with his wife and Edwin Stanton and headed towards the firing. Lincoln's adventures at the front nearly made him the most famous casualty of the battle.

Lincoln arrived at Fort Stevens and decided to climb up on the ramparts to look over the battlefield. All day, Confederate sharpshooter fire from out in the fields had forced the troops inside the fort to keep their heads down. Now, as the president of the United States climbed up, it would be no different. Standing next to Lincoln, a regimental surgeon soon tumbled backwards, shot in the leg. Lincoln quickly clambered back down behind the protection of Fort Stevens's walls.

Historical lore of the battle says that Oliver W. Holmes, future associate justice of the Supreme Court, yelled at Lincoln, "Get down you fool!"—

but it's likely just that: lore. Lincoln's near-miss is also usually accredited as the only time a sitting president ventured onto a battlefield, but President James Madison previously had found himself uncomfortably close to advancing British forces at the battle of Bladensburg in August 1814.

Lincoln's near-miss marked the high point of the fighting at Fort Stevens on July 12. With darkness and the conclusion of fighting, Early began to pull his men back, ending the two-day battle outside Washington that resulted in some 600 casualties.

Not all his soldiers were happy to go. As one Confederate wrote, "for the lack of the dash of a [Stonewall] Jackson, Washington was saved from destruction and Abe Lincoln was reserved for a martyr."

As the Confederates retreated from Silver Spring, they spared that home under orders of Major General Breckinridge, a close friend in the pre-war years of Francis Blair. But the Confederates eagerly burned the nearby home of Montgomery Blair. While Early denied giving orders for the building's destruction, he asserted that "retaliation was justified by previous acts of the enemy," and was more concerned that the burning structure would give away his retreating army's position.

As he led his army away from Fort Stevens, Early looked to one of his staff officers, Henry Kyd Douglas, and said, "Major, we haven't taken Washington, but we've scared Abe Lincoln like hell!"

"Yes, General," Douglas answered, "but this afternoon when that Yankee line moved out against us, I think some other people were scared blue as hell's brimstone!"

"That's true," Early retorted, "but it won't appear in history!"

Evading Union pursuit, Jubal Early brought his army safely across the Potomac, back into Virginia, on July 14.

Early's invasion was over.

Conclusion

CHAPTER TWELVE

"The annual expedition of Confederate forces into Maryland and Pennsylvania has been inaugurated this year at about the usual time," the *Army and Navy Journal* editorialized on July 16, 1864, two days after Early's retreat. "The uniformity of the enemy's appearance around Harper's Ferry should now be nearly sufficient . . . to furnish the July almanac makers with another 'About this time may be expected.'"

Beyond giving fodder for a tongue-in-cheek editorial, what were the ramifications of Early's invasion, and the battle of Monocacy specifically?

For Maj. Gen. Lew Wallace, at least at first, the battle of Monocacy resulted in his dismissal. Major General Henry Halleck had always hated Wallace and what the citizen-soldier represented: amateur soldiers leading troops rather than West Point educated men like Halleck. With Wallace's defeat at Monocacy, Halleck had a solid excuse to get rid of Wallace, and he did not hesitate to do so. On July 11, even as Washington fretted about its safety and officers looked under every crevice for possible troops to send to the front, Halleck wrote orders replacing Wallace with Maj. Gen. Edward O. C. Ord. Wallace kept his administrative position in Baltimore but had his military command, the VIII Corps, stripped away. Incredulous, Wallace nonetheless shored up Baltimore's defenses in wake of that city's fear of the Johnson-Gilmor Raid.

Halleck's personal victory over Wallace was

Dedicated on the 50th anniversary of the battle of Monocacy, the United Daughters of the Confederacy's monument commemorates the Confederate victory and overlooks the Best farm, where sharp skirmishing took place. (cm)

The fields that played host to the battle of Monocacy were already familiar scenes in the Civil War by 1864. Perhaps most famously, in 1862 Robert E. Lee made his headquarters near the Best farm during the campaign that culminated in the battle of Antietam. Near the Best farm were lost the famous Special Orders #191, a blueprint to Lee's campaign discovered by soldiers from the 27th Indiana. (cm)

short lived, though. It did not take long for people to understand the importance of Wallace's stand at Monocacy. "Our fight at Monocacy, although it resulted in our being compelled to fall back with considerable loss, yet certainly was of very great importance," wrote James Read, serving on Ricketts's staff, in a letter home. "Our resistance delayed them probably 48 hours in their march to Washington, and thus enabled the old troops to arrive there, before the rebels attacked." Early's force were not quite delayed the 48 hours Read cited, but the fight at Monocacy did slow the Confederate forces to allow reinforcements to be brought to Washington's defenses. Others came to the same conclusion about Monocacy's importance, including Montgomery Blair, smarting over the burning of his home. According to Halleck, who protested to Lincoln, Blair had said that "the officers in command about Washington are poltroons. . . . General Wallace was in comparison with them far better as he would at least fight." Lincoln shrugged off Halleck's protest.

Halleck soon bore the brunt of criticism that came following the Union invasion. "But how can Stanton have any confidence in Halleck, who cannot command even three broomsticks?" a Washington diarist wondered. "As for Lincoln, he must consider Halleck to be his military clown."

Even Ulysses S. Grant, who himself performed

less than spectacularly in response to the invasion, piled against Halleck when he suggested to Secretary of War Stanton that Halleck would be the perfect fit for an administrative role on the Pacific Coast. But both Grant and Halleck were to blame for the close call; both of them had waited too long to send reinforcements, instead opting to wait and hope that General David Hunter could get back from West Virginia in time to trap Early.

In the midst of the bombardment against Halleck, Lew Wallace was reinstated to command of the VIII Corps on July 28, 1864. He could not help but write to a family member of the irony of the situation with him and Halleck: "I am now really getting more credit than I deserve—so it always is with our people—the dog they kicked yesterday becomes the hero today—vice versa."

Lew Wallace found himself second-in-command to the military commission that tried the conspirators in Lincoln's assassination—a trial that ended in four conspirators hanging in July 1865 (above). About a month and a half after the Lincoln conspirators hanged, Wallace sat in command of the commission that tried Henry Wirz, commandant of the Confederate prison at Andersonville—a trial that also ended in a hanging, this time in November 1865 (below). Wirz reminded Wallace of a cat "when the animal is excited by the scent of prey." (loc)(loc)

William "Billy the Kid" Bonney took up much of Wallace's time during his tenure as the territorial governor of New Mexico from 1878-1881. Bonney was shot and killed four months after Wallace resigned the post. (loc)

But was Wallace "getting more credit" than he deserved? In his official report, Wallace wrote that he wished to see a monument on the battlefield: "which I propose to write: 'These men died to save the National Capital, and they did save it.'" One of the Union brigade commanders at Monocacy, Col. Matthew McClennan, wrote, "The battle of Monocacy was one of great spirit and importance, and in my belief saved the city of Washington from the raves of the enemy."

Beyond the soldiers who fought at Monocacy, officials also knew the battle's importance. A Treasury Department clerk wrote that Washington's "capture and possession for a day would have been disastrous to the cause of the Union. Early would have seized the money in the Treasury, the archives of the departments, the immense supplies of clothing, arms, and ammunition in store."

And what of Lincoln's reelection prospects? At a time when morale had nearly bottomed out due to the horrendous casualties of the Overland Campaign and the slow contest for the city of Atlanta, a Confederate force in Washington, even for a brief time, would have undoubtedly delivered Lincoln's reelection bid a devastating, if not mortal, wound.

Ulysses S. Grant offered a final word for Lew Wallace in 1885. Over twenty years after the battle of Shiloh, he and Wallace had finally started to patch up their relationship. Grant struggled to finish his memoirs before throat cancer killed him and, writing about Early's repulse outside Washington, opined, "There is no telling how much this result was contributed by General Lew Wallace's leading what might well

Jubal Early's new opponent for the fall of 1864 in the Shenandoah Valley was Maj. Gen. Philip Sheridan. Egotistical and not hesitant to step on others on his way to the top, Sheridan was given command of the operations in the Valley by Ulysses S. Grant. The troops who fought under Wallace at Monocacy soon found themselves in hard fighting under Sheridan. (loc)

The battle of Third Winchester (top right) on September 19, 1864, marked Early's first fight with Sheridan—a Federal victory that left Early retreating up the Valley. More battles followed, culminating with the battle of Cedar Creek (bottom right) exactly one month after Winchester. Defeated in all the battles against Sheridan, Early's forces were broken and the Confederacy's hold of the Shenandoah gone forever. Robert Rodes and Stephen Ramseur, who had been so beneficial to Early on his march against Washington, were killed at Winchester and Cedar Creek, respectively. (loc)(loc)

be considered almost a forlorn hope. If Early had been but one day earlier he might have entered the capital before the arrival of the reinforcements I had sent. Whether the delay caused by the battle [of Monocacy] amounted to a day or not, General Wallace contributed on this occasion, by the defeat of the troops under him a greater benefit to the cause than often falls to the lot of a commander of an equal force to render by means of victory."

*   *   *

What of Jubal Early—how did his campaign fare? Depending on what sources one looks at, Early's campaign had different objectives, but no matter what those objectives, Early's invasion had a mixed-bag of results. In forwarding Early's official report, Robert E. Lee wrote to the Confederate Secretary of War, James Seddon, that with the invasion "it was hoped that by threatening Washington and Baltimore Genl. Grant would be compelled either to weaken himself so much for their protection as to afford us an opportunity to attack him, or that he might be induced to attack us." In that regard, Early

After the Civil War ended, Jubal Early temporarily fled the country rather than surrender. Here he sits in Havana, Cuba, with Thomas Turner, the former commandant of the infamous Libby Prison in Richmond, who had fled to avoid prosecution for the ill-treatment of Union prisoners. (je)

The first memorialization of the battle of Monocacy came in 1907 when surviving members of the regiment dedicated the 14th New Jersey monument. Unlike the usual battlefield monument that marks where a regiment fought, the New Jerseyans' statue is a general marker of their time both on garrison duty at the Monocacy Junction as well as during the battle. Because of their experience near the railroad hub, the 14th earned the nickname "The Monocacy Regiment." (rq)

succeeded—both the VI and XIX Corps were sent to Washington, decreasing the total Federal forces at Petersburg. But nothing came from that change in the status quo—the daily grind of the siege lines continued unabated, and now, in the Shenandoah Valley, Early found himself hounded by those same Federal corps sent to protect Washington.

And then there is the matter of what Early himself said was the objective of the invasion. While still forming his forces in the aftermath of beating Hunter, Early had written to Lee that he planned to "threaten Washington and if I find the opportunity—to take it." Even after being stopped at Harpers Ferry, Early's next move was to advance over South Mountain and "I then move on Washington." In Early's mind, this would be an invasion to capture the enemy's capital regardless of what troops were sent against him. With that objective as the end point, Early's invasion failed. The objective of capturing Washington, D.C., also raised Early's move north beyond the diminutive raid that it is too-often depicted as, and instead moved it into the category of an invasion.

Two officers have not been credited until recent scholarship in their role in defeating Early. They are Union generals Franz Sigel and Max Weber. Lew Wallace managed to delay Early's force for one day at Monocacy; Sigel and Weber stopped Early for three days. Their stand atop Maryland Heights at Harpers Ferry changed the entire scenario; rather than having the Potomac River act as a conduit straight to Washington, Early instead needed more time to go through the South Mountain passes and then battle through Frederick and across the Monocacy. The losses at Harpers Ferry may have been small, but the fighting there also finally alerted Federal officials about the seriousness of the invasion north. Of the two, Sigel certainly had his faults and, no matter what, will always bear the defeat at New Market, but his stand at Harpers Ferry alongside Weber deserves more recognition for what it accomplished.

*   *   *

Lew Wallace did not fight another battle after Monocacy. In 1865, he sat on commissions that tried both the conspirators involved in the Lincoln Assassination and Henry Wirz, the commandant of the infamous Andersonville prisoner-of-war camp. Out of the army, Wallace served as New Mexico's territorial governor in the 1870s before, in 1880, publishing the novel that would make him known worldwide. *Ben-Hur: A Tale of Christ* became an almost instant bestseller, making Wallace tens of thousands. In 1881, Wallace took a position as ambassador to the Ottoman Empire. On February 15, 1905, he died at the age of 77. He is buried at his childhood home in Crawfordsville, Indiana.

Fighting with George Davis on the skirmish line, Judson Spofford from the 10th Vermont was initially believed to be the last surviving Union veteran from the battle of Monocacy. After the war, he moved to Idaho and, upon his death in 1938, was buried in Arlington Cemetery. However, he predeceased the genuine last-known surviving Union soldier, Horace Anderson, who died two months after Spofford. (jh)

Unlike Wallace, Jubal Early still had lots of fighting to go before peace in 1865. His command in the Shenandoah Valley during the fall of 1864 saw three straight large defeats at Third Winchester, Fisher's Hill, and Cedar Creek. A fourth defeat in 1865 at Waynesboro led to his removal from command. After the war, rather than surrender, Early fled to Mexico and then Canada. Returning to Virginia in 1869, Early was always critical of the Federal administration and became a leading figure in the budding Lost Cause movement. He, like Wallace, died at the age of 77, albeit in 1894. Early is buried in Lynchburg, Virginia, site of his most important victory.

The veterans of Monocacy continued fighting as well. On both sides, they fought until the war's conclusion in 1865. Some returned to Monocacy, like Ervin Dunbar, who walked the overgrown battlefield in 1913. A soldier in the 10th Vermont, Dunbar "called at the Thomas house and got water where 49 years before we would not let McCausland's and Gordon's men drink." Others went to dedicate monuments to fallen comrades. The last known veteran of the battle, Horace Anderson, who served as an artillerist in Frederick Alexander's Baltimore Light Artillery, died in 1937—three years after the battlefield's designation as a National Park Site.

The Civilian's Experience at the Battle of Monocacy

APPENDIX A
BY RYAN T. QUINT

The civilians living along the Monocacy River on what would become the battlefield on July 9, 1864, were no strangers to war. It seemed that the opposing armies were constantly coming through their yards or setting up temporary headquarters on their way to battlefields down the road.

But on July 9, the armies didn't move on. They stayed, and they fought for hours along the winding river, leaving the families huddled in basements. When the Confederates finally marched away victoriously, they left a landscape forever changed.

The families most impacted by the battle were the Bests, Worthingtons, Thomases, and Gambrills. Other nearby homes and families certainly saw and heard the contending armies, but the families mentioned above found themselves surrounded by the battle, consumed by it, even potential casualties of it.

Located on the north side of the Monocacy, the Best farm became a position for Confederate artillery and sharpshooters. Belonging to Charles Trail, who lived in Frederick, the Best farm got its name from the family that tenanted on the land, working the farm in exchange for staying there. David Best had started the arrangement, but by the time of the battle, his eldest son, John Best, had taken over much of the work.

On the morning of July 9, the Bests tried to gather as much of their crops as they could even as the two armies came into contact. The crop harvest came to a sudden end as John Massie's Fluvanna Artillery rolled up next to their home and began to unlimber. Hustling to their basement, the Bests took shelter as Union cannons

Looking from the gun line of the Monroe Artillery at the Worthington farm towards the location of the Federal battle line on the other side of the trees. Such proximity to homes put the citizens of the Monocacy River extremely close to the fighting. (rq)

John and Margaret Best found their farming on the morning of July 9, 1864, interrupted by the outbreak of fighting. The property they rented from Charles Trail was damaged badly during the battle, including the loss of a barn. By the time of the 1870 census, the Bests had recovered from some of the Civil War damages, and their estate was valued at $6,000. (mnb)(mnb)

John Worthington purchased "Clifton" in 1862. His family watched as the battle unfolded around their property, leaving the dead, wounded, and debris. (mnb)

destroyed their barn and skirmishers popped away at each other. Emerging from their home, the Bests rebuilt their barn and lived on, John Best working the land until the late 1880s.

Crossing the Monocacy River, the first home Confederate troops came into contact with was Clifton, the Worthington home. The fighting around the Worthington farm is told in Chapters 7-9, but for the Worthington family, like the Bests, the day started with last-minute crop harvesting. Glenn Worthington later remembered, "The crop of wheat which had ripened under the summer skies, on the Worthington and Thomas farms, as well as elsewhere in the community had been reaped and was standing in shocks over the wheat fields, ready to be gathered into barns or put into stacks."

Utilizing "a few" slaves that he owned, John Worthington hurriedly went from shock to shock, hauling and loading them into a small wagon. But as the cannonading grew louder from the other side of the river, Worthington called an end to the haul. He ordered that the family horses be untethered and brought to nearby Sugar Loaf Mountain so that they might avoid being captured. As his slaves went off, Worthington turned to protecting his family. He "had heavy two-inch boards put

"Araby," the oldest surviving home on the Monocacy battlefield, was originally constructed in the 1780s for a wealthy landowner, James Marshall. By the Civil War, C. K. Thomas lived in the home with his family and took shelter in the cellar. (ts)

across the cellar windows . . . also he had several tubs and a barrel filled with water, placed in the cellar."

With fighting intensifying, the Worthingtons took in Frank Mantz, a telegraph operator for the B&O, and his family. Taking cover in the cellar, the families, especially young Glenn watched and listened as first John McClausland's and then John Gordon's men came up to fight.

Through one of the windows of the Worthington's basement, young Glenn Worthington watched the battle of Monocacy unfold. The Worthingtons were just one family forced to take shelter as the fighting began along the banks of the Monocacy River. (cm)

At the tail end of the battle, John Worthington nearly became a casualty of the battle. Exiting his home, Worthington saw Maj. Gen. John C. Breckinridge, "a very distinguished person in his day and generation," and went to shake Breckinridge's hand. As they did so, a last rifle shot of defiance zipped by, fired from the retreating Federals. "Mr. Worthington, it is not safe for you to be here," Breckinridge said. "Bullets are still flying and you might be seriously hurt." Contesting that it was just as dangerous for Breckinridge as he, Worthington surrendered the point when Breckinridge responded, "It is my duty to be here and not yours." Glenn remembered his father "often told the story of the little incident, always with manifest respect and admiration for the distinguished and dignified Southern statesman and soldier."

While John Worthington escaped injury, his son Glenn did not. At the end of the battle, Confederate forces used the Worthington farm as a staging area for wounded soldiers as well as destroying excess weapons behind the home. For the latter, soldiers gathered muskets or rifles, covered them in kindling, and then lit a fire. After the blaze, Glenn Worthington saw a bayonet and, writing in the third person, explained, he "desired [it] for his own purposes." But as he dragged the bayonet out, the young boy accidentally shoved a hot coal towards a paper cartridge that exploded with a flash. "Then there was a yelp, akin to the rebel yell, and some pitying Confederate picked the boy up in his arms and carried him, blinded and yelling, to the house." The blinding proved only temporary, though, "and the disfigurement was not noticeable at the end of a year."

Moving on from the Worthington farm, the battle descended on the Thomas farm, Araby,

Maj. Peter Vredenburgh served with the 14th New Jersey at Monocacy. At the height of the battle, he ran into the cellar to check on the Thomas family, who had befriended him when he was stationed near the Monocacy in 1862. Vredenburgh survived the battle but was later killed at the battle of Third Winchester. (mnb)

James Gambrill sits with his family after the Civil War. During the battle of Monocacy, Gambrill and his wife, Antoinette, only had two children as opposed to the eight seen in the photograph. Antoinette and the two sons hid in the cellar of the Thomas farm while James stayed near his mill. (mnb)

James Gambrill's mill was originally a two-story structure. The building was adapted and used as a visitor center for the National Park Service starting in the 1990s until the park's new visitor center opened in 2007. (mnb)

belonging to Christian Keefer Thomas. Like his neighbors, Thomas also spent the morning of the battle hauling in wheat shocks. Sending his horses along with John Worthington's slaves to Sugar Loaf Mountain, Thomas looked to the protection of his family. Taking shelter in Araby's basement, Thomas joined his wife and three children, as well as a family friend, Mamie Tyler, and a black female slave. Soon adding to the crowd in the basement was the wife of James Gambrill, Antoinette, and her two sons.

As the fighting began to swing towards the Thomas farm, Maj. Peter Vredenburgh of the 14th New Jersey ran into the home to check on the family. Before joining the VI Corps, the New Jersey men had been posted at the Monocacy Junction, and during the posting, Vredenburgh had become closely acquainted with the Thomases. Running into the home and downstairs, Vredenburgh found the family and their fellow refugees "in the cellar frightened to death." Vredenburgh rushed through the house "and locked the drawers—some of the doors and brought downstairs a basket of silver that they had packed up." Making sure the family was settled in place for the coming fight, Vredenburgh prepared to return to the 14th New Jersey, but the occupants of the basement "hung on me and wanted me to stay," and asked him to bring a wounded Confederate left over from McCausland's attacks

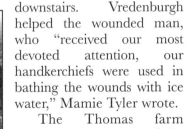

downstairs. Vredenburgh helped the wounded man, who "received our most devoted attention, our handkerchiefs were used in bathing the wounds with ice water," Mamie Tyler wrote.

The Thomas farm became the epicenter of the battle's worst fighting. "You can imagine how strange the sounds outside of those walls," Mamie Tyler later wrote. "Minnie balls slashed the shrubbery while the larger missiles of war's fearful instruments twisted huge limbs from the trees, leveled down chimneys and tore out an angle of the house." After the Confederate victory, the Thomas family climbed out and helped the wounded that now surrounded their home.

Before and during the battle's chaotic and bloody finish, the Thomases also worried for three of their missing family and friends—Samuel Thomas, Christian's son; Julius Anderson, fiancé of Christian's daughter Alice; and Hugh Gatchell, Mamie Tyler's fiancé. They had made their way to Araby for Independence Day, but in the confusion of Lew Wallace trying to get troops to defend the Monocacy River, the three men found themselves drafted on the spot and impressed into one of Erastus Tyler's regiments. On July 9, as the fighting got underway, an officer spoke to the three: "Young men, if you should be captured fighting in civilian clothes, you are likely to be shot. General Wallace is now at some distance and I advise you to get away from here as fast as you can." The three listened without a second's notice and ran towards James Gambrill's mill.

Gambrill had stayed behind at his mill to protect the property after he sent his wife and children to Araby. He sat on his porch talking to General Ricketts as Ricketts's division lounged on the Gambrill property, drawing rations. But when Confederate guns from across the river opened fired, Ricketts's men formed up, and Gambrill and the three men ran for cover in the protection of the mill's complex. Some of them thought it a good idea to seek cover in the mill's waterwheel, but soon "their most fearful apprehension was that the huge overshot waterwheel might start revolving while they were taking shelter there, but during the three hours and more of their concealment, it remained motionless and they came forth, finally, unscathed." It was good that the wheel hadn't moved because soon the grounds of the Gambrill Mill churned to pieces by the dozens of Confederate cannon and Frederick Alexander's battery firing back—escape from the churning wheel and battle both would have been impossible.

With the exception of Glenn Worthington's self-inflicted wound, all of the civilians came away unhurt from the battle of Monocacy. Each of their stories—like those of thousands of soldiers who fought there—is full of drama and harrowing examples of survival. Then, just as quickly as it had come with all its fury, the war moved on.

Visiting his family in early July, Samuel Thomas (center), was forced into service with the Union army along with his friends Julius Anderson (left) and Hugh Gatchell (right). On the morning of the battle, a Union staff officer let the three of them go, and they subsequently hid with James Gambrill on the mill property. (mnb)

The Ransom of Frederick

APPENDIX B
BY RYAN T. QUINT

On July 9, 1864, at around 8 a.m., William G. Cole, the mayor of Frederick, received a pair of notes. Both came from the headquarters of Lt. Gen. Jubal Early, who had set up in the home of Dr. Richmond Hammond while Confederate forces moved through the town. As Cole read the messages, he called the town's municipal government together.

"We require of the Mayor and town authorities $200,000 in current money for the use of this army," the first message started. "This contribution may be supplied by furnishing the medical department with $50,000 in stores at current prices; the Commissary department with stores to the same amount; the Ordnance department with the same and the Quartermaster's department with a like amount," the demand conditioned.

If the first levy for $200,000 was not enough, the second message brought another order—this time from Early's Chief of Commissary, Wells Hawks, demanding 500 barrels of flour, 3,000 pounds of coffee, 3,000 pounds of salt, 6,000 pounds of sugar, and finishing off with 20,000 pounds of bacon.

As Jubal Early had endorsed the messages and sent them off to Cole, the commanding general made sure to be clear the demands were to be taken seriously. Looking to Dr. Hammond's wife, Mary, Early said, "if the demand is granted, very good, if not, Frederick will be reduced to ashes. We do this in retaliation for similar acts done by the Federal forces within our borders." As if to soften the blow of the ultimatum, Early assured, "You need not fear as timely warning will be given you to leave with your family."

Gathering the town council and others, Cole began to work on a response to the two messages. The first of their problems to address was the fact that a $200,000 levy—or ransom, pending Early's decision to burn the town— would financially devastate the town's

The home of Dr. Richard Hammond, where Jubal Early made his headquarters early on July 9, 1864, no longer exists. One can still go to the site of the building, however, at the northwest corner of Second and Market Streets. (rq)

Involving himself in politics starting in the 1830s, William G. Cole served as mayor of Frederick from 1859–65. (hsfc)

8,000 citizens. Drafting a reply, Cole and the others wrote, "The assessment imposed by your order will take from the citizens of this place nearly one tenth of the taxable property of the city." Pushing further, the town's leaders continued, "In view therefore of the great and onerous burthen thrown upon our citizens, many of whom are indigent and unable to bear the loss, and as the assessment made in other places in Maryland is relatively much less than that imposed upon our city, we respectfully request you to reconsider and abate the said assessment." Signing their names, the town's leaders sent their request back to Early.

In response to Early, Frederick's leaders referenced "other places in Maryland" that Confederate forces had ransomed before coming to town in an argument to lower the levy. On July 6 the town of Hagerstown had been ransomed for $20,000, and on July 8 the citizens of Middletown faced a demand for $5,000.

Word had clearly trickled down the Catoctin Mountain to Frederick, letting the town leaders know what was coming their way. So, at face value, asking for a lower sum for Frederick was not a bad idea, but what the town leaders did not know was that one of the ransoms, Hagerstown, had been poorly managed, and the Confederates were not going to make the same mistake twice.

Brigadier General John McCausland and his cavalry had been responsible for gathering Hagerstown's ransom on July 6. McCausland had orders from Early to demand $200,000 from

Confederate cavalry looted stores in Hagerstown on July 6, three days before Monocacy. They also made a decimal-point mistake that cost them $180,000—an error they would not repeat in Frederick. (loc)

PILLAGING AT HAGERSTOWN.

Two of Early's four commissioners assigned to get the ransom from Frederick were Wells Hawks (left) and William Allan (right). Both men had served as members of Stonewall Jackson's staff before his death in 1863. (cv) (usahec)

Hagerstown's populace, but when McCausland gave the ransom, somehow a decimal had been misunderstood. The $200,000 ransom became $20,000, and with such a fumble, Confederate officers were going to look very closely at Frederick.

Early himself did not see Frederick's town council's reply to the ransom. He had appointed commissioners to act in his stead, and these officers—Lt. Col. William Allan, Maj. Wells Hawks, Maj. John Harmon, and Surgeon Hunter McGuire—dismissed the counter out of hand. The sound of fighting grew to the south, and William Allan later wrote that he thought the town officials delayed "until the issue of the battle with Wallace should be ascertained."

While fighting continued near the railroad junction, Confederate officers waited in Frederick. Major Henry Kyd Douglas, another of Early's staffers, wrote that he "was appointed Provost Marshal of the town," and rode the streets. Catharine Markell, a Southern sympathizer, noted that Douglas, amongst others, "called at noon."

Other Confederates, however, did not prove so hospitable or patient. Diarist Jacob Engelbrecht remembered that the soldiers "stole all the Good horses & cattle, money, bacon, corn, oats &c that they could lay hands on. . . . The Rebs threatened to shoot people if they would not give up their money, horses, &c."

By evening, the Federal troops were in retreat back to Baltimore, and the town leaders in Frederick

For more than 20 years, Marylander Charles Mathias championed the cause of reimbursement for Frederick. In 1986, just as it looked like Frederick would indeed get the money back, Mathias proclaimed "At long last justice has been served." However, like all of Mathias's prior bills, the plan was scrapped. (dod)

could delay no longer. To furnish the $200,000, five banks were called upon, who gave up the money only after being promised by the town to be paid back. The resulting loans would haunt Frederick for nearly a century.

Table 1: Paying the Ransom of Frederick

Bank	Amount Provided
Frederick Town Savings Institution	$64,000
Central Bank	$44,000
Frederick County Bank	$33,000
Franklin Savings Bank	$31,000
The Farmers and Mechanics Bank	$28,000

Around 5:00 p.m., nine hours after first getting the demand, the town leaders had the money delivered to Maj. J. R. Braithwaite, who loaded the cash-filled wicker baskets into a wagon and then wrote out a receipt. As historian Benjamin F. Cooling notes, "In all, Early's ransom reduced Frederick coffers by one-quarter of their capital."

With their personal mission accomplished, the officers on Early's staff celebrated. Alexander "Sandie" Pendleton, who had spent part of his childhood living in Frederick, led William Allan, Wells Hawks, and John Harman to a restaurant for a dinner more upscale than usual. "I recall especially the ice cream seemed delicious to us who had had no such delicacies for a long time," Allan later wrote. "The owner gave us champagne too & we had a good time for an hour."

The Confederate army rumbled out of Frederick on July 10, leaving the town to deal with the repercussion of the battle and the ransom. Gradually paying the five banks back, Frederick's citizenry also had to cope with interest that piled atop the loans, so that by 1951, when the last payment was fulfilled, the Confederate levy actually cost the town some $600,000.

The city of Frederick eventually paid its entire debt off, although starting shortly after the end of the Civil War, officials tried to get the United States government to reimburse the city. On February 10, 1873, John Ritchie, serving in the U.S. House of Representatives, put forth H.R. 3894, which promoted "To appropriate three hundred thousand dollars for the relief of Frederick City." Ritchie's resolution went nowhere. A similar bill introduced in the 43rd Congress was tabled by the Committee on War Claims in 1876.

The inability to get reimbursed continued in the Twentieth Century. Maryland politician Charles Mathias, elected in 1961 as a member of the House of Representatives, proposed his first bill for Frederick that same year. Then, elected to the U.S. Senate in 1969, Mathias continued his crusade for Frederick, re-introducing the "Frederick Reimbursement Bill" every single year. Finally, in 1986, it looked like Mathias's personal crusade would end in victory as a specification for a spending bill looked to pay Frederick back. But then, it too, like all others before it, was scrapped. Mathias left office a year later.

To date, 152 years after the ransom, Frederick has not received a cent of reimbursement from the United States government.

Medical Care and the Battle of Monocacy

APPENDIX C
BY JAKE WYNN

When the armies marched away from Frederick, Maryland, in the aftermath of battle in July 1864, they left behind a landscape marred by the day of terrible fighting. These scenes had been witnessed before in Maryland, but never this close to the 8,000 residents of the city known for its cluster of church steeples. The horrible sights and smells of a battlefield had before seemed distant to the residents of Frederick, over mountains or across borders in Virginia and at Gettysburg, Pennsylvania. Now they were right here, just three short miles from the heart of their city.

With the approach of Confederate raiders, many citizens evacuated the city, not wishing to discover the darkest heart of war. For the surgeons at work on the sick inside Frederick's United States General Hospital #1 on the city's south side, the arrival of Confederate forces in July 1864 marked an immense influx of patients with horrific injuries. This was not the first time these surgeons in blue were tested by gore of brotherly war, but the proximity this time would be unsettlingly close.

Yet the story of Frederick in the Civil War relates very closely with the rapidly-evolving narrative of battlefield medicine. The city received its first large war-time hospital late in 1861, when Union forces first arrived in the area in large numbers. By 1862, army surgeons had turned the grounds of the Frederick Agricultural Society into the growing United States General Hospital #1 with room for hundreds of patients. Two sturdy stone buildings, originally constructed as barracks during the Revolutionary War period stood at its heart. These "Hessian" barracks had seen war before, but nothing like what arrived in September 1862.

Located within an old furniture store that was also used by an embalmer, the National Museum of Civil War Medicine in Frederick tells the story of medical knowledge during the war. Visitors can tour through its multiple floors of exhibits and follow the footsteps of wounded soldiers from the battlefield to hospitals. (cm)

Maj. Jonathan Letterman, seated first from left with his staff (above), headed the Army of the Potomac's Medical Department. Under Letterman's direction, the Medical Department transformed into an extremely capable branch of the military service. Below, one can start to see how large an operation the evacuation of the wounded required, with hundreds of ambulances and even more horses. (loc)(loc)

In that month, the eyes of the world turned to Frederick. With armies passing down its streets, residents prepared for whatever might come next. The Army of the Potomac's Medical Director, Maj. Jonathan Letterman, chose the city and its spacious public buildings as future hospitals for the wounded that would surely come from this Maryland Campaign. And they came—10,000 strong. Wounded and sick men poured into the city, dozens of ambulances arriving each day in the wake of the battles of South Mountain and Antietam. This horror prepared the citizens of Frederick for what came in July 1864.

"At the Barracks yesterday I saw at least 500 Rebel wounded & also of course prisoners," wrote resident Jacob Engelbrecht on July 12, just days after the engagement. "Many had limbs amputated[.] I saw one operation of the amputation of the left leg of a Union soldier by Doctor Wier of United States Hospital. It took about 20 minutes."

The prolific diarist captured this moment, in the immediate aftermath of the battle as patients were being brought off the battlefield just a few miles away. Not only the living, though, but the fallen as well. "There were 15 Rebel & 5 Union (dead) buried yesterday afternoon (Sunday July 10th) about 10 o'clock AM," he added.

The Battle of Monocacy can be seen in the midst of a medical transformation within the military medical system as well. Prior to the ascendency of Letterman to command of the medical department of the Army of the Potomac in the summer of 1862, the evacuation of patients from the battlefield was a disorganized mess. Major Letterman ushered in the era of triage within American military circles. His evacuation system and overhaul of the ambulance service served the Union Army well in the massive battles fought between 1862 and the end of 1863. Letterman took a broken system and turned it into an efficient, lifesaving organization that brought triage to the American battlefield. For the first time, a wounded soldier's care was organized and monitored from the instant he fell on the battlefield to the moment he was wheeled into a general hospital in a northern city. The Union Army's medical care was never the same. The battles of Antietam, Fredericksburg, Chancellorsville, and Gettysburg saw Letterman directly oversee the treatment and transportation of thousands of wounded and sick soldiers.

By the summer of 1864, although Letterman was no longer in command, his overhaul of military medicine within the Union Army had been enshrined as United States law on March 1, 1864, forever altering the course of American battlefield medicine and leaving behind a system that remains in place today.

With its testing at the previous battles from 1862 to 1863, Letterman's system of evacuating wounded from the battlefield was tried and true. Soldiers wounded at Monocacy were retrieved and brought back to aid stations on both sides of the battlefield. First aid was rendered, and transportation procured to the rear to field hospitals occupying homes, barns, and tents close to the battlefield. Here, surgeons and their assistants worked diligently to save lives amid often horrendous conditions. In this age before germ theory, unclean instruments and hands led to rampant infections, and misery followed.

From the field hospitals, patients were to be evacuated to a more permanent facility. Luckily for those wounded on both sides at Monocacy on July 9, Frederick's U.S. General Hospital #1 had been untouched by the Confederate marauding in the city and had 2,500 to 3,000 beds available. "It had on hand a full equipment of instruments, medical and quartermaster supplies which were not touched by the enemy," reported surgeon Robert Weir years later. This full load of supplies would prove to be helpful for the influx of patients that came in following the engagement on the ninth.

The *Frederick Examiner* recorded that on Saturday, July 23, the hospital had 1,221 patients within its care. That figure nearly doubled its pre-battle quota. By the next week, an additional 575 patients were admitted to the wards of U.S. General Hospital #1. That week also demonstrates that repairs had been made to the damaged Baltimore & Ohio Railroad, as 565 patients were transferred out of the hospital and on to the larger general hospitals in cities like Baltimore and Washington.

The experience of Frederick in prior military campaigns made it ideally placed to handle wounded soldiers in July 1864. The hospital would remain a repository for Monocacy's casualties for months following the battle and would continue taking patients from the

Letterman's first test came with the battle of Antietam, September 17, 1862, a fight that took place not far from Frederick. By the end of the fighting, thousands of wounded needed attention. The maimed flooded into Frederick, requiring the use of almost all public buildings. (loc)

One of the buildings used after Antietam was the Hessian Barracks, known during the Civil War as U.S. General Hospital Number One. Originally built in the late 1770s, the buildings were used to house Hessian prisoners of war from the American Revolution. Adapted for use as a hospital complex, it housed all of the wounded from the battle of Monocacy in 1864. A soldier detailed to the hospital as a nurse wrote, "The people here are very kind to the sick and wounded in bringing good things to eat." (nmcwm)

subsequent campaigns. As Ulysses S. Grant and Philip Sheridan worked out a strategy for the Shenandoah Valley Campaign of 1864, Frederick's U.S. General Hospital #1 prepared to take on the sick and wounded from Sheridan's enterprise through the rest of 1864.

The legacy of Civil War medicine in Frederick is continued to this day by the operations of the National Museum of Civil War Medicine. Located on East Patrick Street in downtown Frederick, the museum tells the complex and comparatively unknown story of the surgeons and medical officials who fought battles with death and disease long after the guns fell silent. The story of the Battle of Monocacy would not be complete without the addition of the medical story. The struggles of those struck down on the fields south of Frederick would stretch into the months and years that followed.

JAKE WYNN is a native Pennsylvanian and historian at the National Museum of Museum of Civil War Medicine in Frederick, Maryland.

"Utterly Impossible For Man or Horse to Accomplish": The Johnson-Gilmor Raid

APPENDIX D
BY PHILLIP S. GREENWALT

Tired, frustrated, dusty, and grimy, Confederate Brig. Gen. Bradley T. Johnson trudged into Lt. Gen. Jubal A. Early's headquarters in Middletown, Maryland, during the evening of July 8, 1864. Whatever renewed spirit he'd had being back on his native soil in Maryland and within miles of his birthplace had been dashed the day before. The over cautiousness of his commanding officer, Maj. Gen. Robert Ransom, had robbed him of the chance of capturing or ransoming the staunchly Unionist Western Maryland town of Frederick.

What awaited Johnson when he came to face to face with Early must have struck the Marylander as a cruel joke—an order that highlighted the desperation of the invasion of Maryland and underscored the drastic shortage of manpower the Confederacy faced by the summer of 1864.

The task Early laid before Johnson that night was "utterly impossible," according to the cavalry officer. He was to strike out with his command, numbering approximately 1,500 cavalry troopers, on an approximately 140-mile venture to the southern tip of Maryland's western Chesapeake Bay shore. His destination: Point Lookout. There, where the Potomac River emptied into the Chesapeake Bay, the fort-turned-prison housed between 10,000 to 12,000 Confederate prisoners—roughly the size of Early's entire infantry force. Johnson was to liberate those prisoners.

Two monuments to Confederate soldiers stand at Point Lookout, Maryland. In the background sits a white marble obelisk constructed in 1876, with the larger obelisk in the foreground completed in 1911. Almost 3,400 Confederate soldiers died during the time Point Lookout served as a prisoner of war camp. (loc)

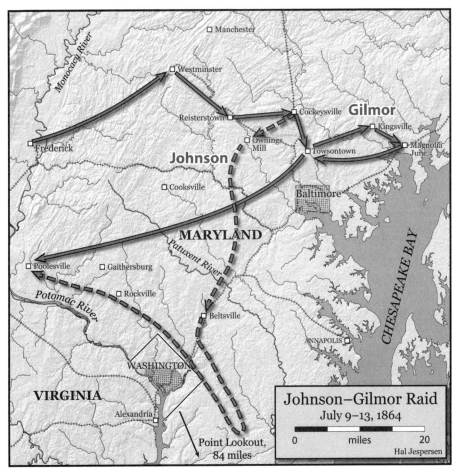

JOHNSON-GILMOR RAID—Leaving Frederick on July 9 while the battle of Monocacy raged, Bradley Johnson and Harry Gilmor's commands rode together until they reached Cockeysville. There, the two forces split with different objectives that included destroying railroad supplies and raising fear in cities like Washington or Baltimore (Gilmour is depicted by the solid line, Johnson by the dotted). The one objective that was not accomplished, however, was the very point of the cavalry raid: the liberation of Point Lookout. When it became clear that Jubal Early's main forces would not get into Washington, the cavalry detachments were recalled.

Johnson's orders called for him to rendezvous with a naval contingent under the command of Commander John Taylor Wood, who would be bringing small arms for the freed soldiers plus marines and sailors to help with the assault on the Union defenses.

If the plan did not seem fantastical enough by this juncture, the next step stretched the bounds of credulity. Johnson was to march the freed soldiers back to Bladensburg, a Maryland town

The target for Bradley Johnson's raid, Point Lookout. Opened as a prisoner of war camp in the aftermath of the battle of Gettysburg in July 1863, by a year later some 15,500 soldiers were imprisoned there. Robert E. Lee hoped to free those men and bring them back into service, negating some of the heavy losses from the bloody spring 1864 fighting. (loc)

to the southeast of Washington, D.C., where they would cross the Potomac River and join up with Early's forces. If Early was by then successful in his planned assault on Washington, further arms could be distributed from the arsenals captured during that engagement.

Besides the 140 miles to get to Point Lookout, Johnson had to travel more than a hundred additional miles to meet back up with the Confederate arm—and he had three days and nights to complete the entire mission. The plan stipulated "four days . . . to campaign nearly three hundred miles, not counting time lost to destroy bridges and railroads," Johnson groused. Although he thought the entire scheme was "utterly impossible for man or horse to accomplish," orders were orders, and he "would do what was possible for men to do." The cavalry would sneak away the next day, July 9, beyond the left flank of the Confederate army while it was at the Monocacy River, and head toward his calvalry's objective.

Riding in Johnson's command was the 1st Maryland Battalion, now under the command

Commander John Taylor Wood was in charge of the contingent of Confederate naval forces who were supposed to help Johnson attack the Federal troops at Point Lookout. Wood's armada would then ferry the prisoners back to Virginia. (nhhc)

of Maj. Harry Gilmor, along with what was left of the 2nd Maryland Cavalry. Gilmor was a native Marylander born near Towsontown—now Towson, Maryland—on January 24, 1838. He had been arrested during the Pratt Street Riots on April 19,

1861, in Baltimore and imprisoned in Fort McHenry. After his release, he travelled south, became a competent cavalry and partisan ranger, and accompanied the Army of Northern Virginia north to Gettysburg in 1863, where he served as provost marshal of the town during the Confederate occupation.

With the sound of guns firing along the banks of Monocacy River on July 9, Johnson, Gilmor, and the rest of the brigade rode eastward to Westminster, Maryland, approximately 25 miles from Frederick.

Harry Gilmor, Johnson's second-in-command during the raid, was involved in some of the war's first bloodshed. On April 19, 1861, as the 6th Massachusetts State Militia marched through the streets of Baltimore, a pro-Secessionist mob attacked them. Racing through the streets, the Massachusetts men opened fire to defend themselves on their way to the railroad station. By the time the fighting in the streets was finished, 16 people were killed and dozens more wounded. Because of his actions, Harry Gilmor was arrested and thrown into jail at Fort McHenry, the same place the Star Spangled Banner was written in 1814. (loc)

After receiving welcomed foodstuffs from pro-Southern Westminster residents, and riding astride a beautiful black mare from a farmer of the area, Gilmor and the Maryland cavalrymen of Johnson's command struck out on their next assignment: to disable the Northern Central Railroad that connected Baltimore to points north. Additionally, telegraph wires that connected the Charm City of Maryland to the Pennsylvania capital of Harrisburg were also to be cut.

Gilmor's men reached the first bridge, over Gunpowder River, located three miles above Cockeysville, Maryland, on the morning of July 10. By mid morning, Johnson's main force, following behind Gilmor, reached the Baltimore County town of Reisterstown, twelve miles to the west. The two Marylanders then reconvened in Cockeysville, where Gilmor received updated orders: With a complement of 135 men, including Gilmor's "own command" who were "present with serviceable horses and fifty of the 1st Maryland," he was to move quickly toward another bridge over the Gunpowder River, this one utilized by the Philadelphia, Wilmington, and Baltimore Railroad.

Although his raiding force was small, Gilmor spread alarm and consternation among Union authorities and civilians in the Baltimore region. When his troopers departed Cockeysville on Sunday, July 12, and made their feint toward Baltimore, hundreds of Union volunteers and militiamen were called to provide defense for numerous fortifications around that city and its namesake county. However, there was not enough time or manpower to guard every potential Rebel target, and when the Southern raiders reached the Gunpowder River at Meredith's Bridge, situated near Towsontown, in Baltimore County, the span was left unguarded.

Gilmour, a Maryland native, stopped at Glen Ellen, his birthplace, and visited his family. The rest of Sunday was spent reliving happier times of yesteryear.

Meanwhile, the rest of the Confederate cavalry raiding force under Johnson slowly made its way out of Cockeysville, then stopped at Hayfield farm, the home of a friend of Johnson's. Scouts were directed to head toward Baltimore to verify the accuracy of intelligence Johnson received.

With speed being essential to reach the Southern prisoners at Point Lookout, the laziness of Sunday afternoon was most striking. Gilmor, however, would recoup some of the time by continuing his movement to Bel Air during the night, and Johnson would soon head for Green Spring Valley to the northwest of Baltimore and, by daybreak, be in sight of Maryland Governor Augustus Bradford's country house. Johnson ordered the estate torched in retaliation for Union forces under Maj. Gen. David Hunter burning Virginia Governor John Letcher's home in Lexington, Virginia, in May of 1864.

On Monday, Johnson's scouts returned from Baltimore with the startling news that transports awaited offshore with Union reinforcements— chiefly the VI and XIX Corps. This news was passed to a messenger who quickly jumped on his horse and sped across country to try to find General Early.

During David Hunter's campaign in the Shenandoah Valley, Union troops had burned the home of Virginia governor John Letcher (above). In retaliation, during his raid, Bradley Johnson ordered the destruction of the home of Maryland's governor, Augustus Bradford (below). (loc)(loc)

Johnson's men frequently stopped trains and pillaged them during their raid through Maryland. During one such stop the Confederate troopers captured Maj. Gen. William B. Franklin. Franklin (left) soon escaped, though, when his captors fell asleep. (fli)(loc)

During this very hot day, a very cool treat awaited the Southern cavaliers as they headed south into Howard County. Near Owings Mills, the Confederates overtook two wagons headed into market, earmarked on the side: "Painter's Ice Cream." Johnson allowed his men to have a treat. Unfamiliar with this new concoction and lacking the proper utensils to consume it, the Southern soldiers used whatever accoutrements were available—slouch hats, blankets, and buckets. A majority of the soldiers had never seen this type of "frozen mush" and were not sure if they liked "frozen vittles."

One poor soldier stuffing his mouth full of ice cream suddenly yelped in pain. He had the proverbial "brain freeze," as it is known today. One of his comrades, finding it amusing, related that the poor Southwestern Virginian "clapped his hand to both sides of his head . . . jumped up and down . . . it hurt so bad he forgot to spit it out." The "buttermilk Rangers and their ice cream" became a light-hearted memory to the survivors of Johnson's cavalrymen after the war.

The rest of that day was spent in typical cavalry raiding fashion and, by evening, Johnson's Confederates encamped close to the county border of Montgomery, situated between Baltimore and

Washington.

Gilmor's men had continued raiding round Baltimore. There, they suffered the only fatality of the raid: Sgt. Eugene Fields was killed by buckshot from a Unionist farmer near the hamlet of Kingsville, on the Bel Air Turnpike that took travelers out of the city. Although the plucky farmer escaped, his dwelling did not.

Gilmor's men arrived at Magnolia Station on the Philadelphia, Wilmington, and Baltimore Railroad that evening and were able to halt two northbound trains. One of the captures that night was Maj. Gen. William Franklin, recently in service out west.

After a short engagement with Union forces near the Gunpowder River Bridge, Gilmor's troopers rode out of Magnolia Station in the later afternoon of Monday in the direction of Baltimore. Meanwhile, a detail was left to keep an eye on the prisoners. Intelligence, by way of a friend, informed Gilmor that Baltimore was heavily fortified, so the cavalier changed course. Instead of heading toward the city, he cut across country. When he met back up with the prisoner-guard, Gilmor was aghast to find his soldiers asleep. The prisoners, including the Confederates' richest prize, Major General Franklin, had escaped while the pickets dozed in the fence rails!

Monday night passed into Tuesday with Confederate cavalry in the corridor around Baltimore and the nation's capital. The next morning, Johnson's men headed toward Beltsville. They were still nearly 80 miles from Point Lookout.

Luckily for the Marylander, that Tuesday saw a messenger from Early approach the column. Johnson was to abort the mission to Point Lookout and instead head toward Early's main force. No explanation was given, as the courier had not been privy to that intelligence. As one historian has noted, this messenger saved Johnson the embarrassment of having to tell the mercurial and hot-tempered Early that he would never achieve the objective.

Johnson's forces quickly moved to rendezvous

with Early, cutting cross country in sight of Union pickets on the defense parapets of Washington, D.C. With the raid at an end, the majority of the rank and file saw the adventure as a success. Supplies, horses, and mules were in tow back to the Confederate army, life and commerce were derailed for days around Baltimore, and no pitched battle had been fought.

At 9:00 p.m. that Tuesday night, Johnson's column found the road from Washington, D.C., through Rockville—the same approach Early used to head toward and retreat back out from the capital. Three hours later, Johnson reported to Early and received his next assignment: assist with the rearguard duties of the other Confederate cavalry. Gilmor—after unsuccessfully trying to find his escaped prisoners—arrived soon thereafter, catching up with Johnson and Early in Poolesville, Maryland, in the vicinity of the Potomac River.

Early's entire campaign was an audacious task from the beginning, and soldiers throughout the Confederacy eagerly sought information. "[W]e are very anxious to hear from Early," one Confederate soldier in the trenches of Petersburg wrote. "I fear he has undertaken more than he can do with his small force, and he is likely to come to grief." In the middle of all the wagging tongues, news of the Point Lookout Plan had leaked, compromising the mission almost from the get-go. Northern newspapers caught wind of the idea and made note that Union authorities would begin transferring prisoners from Point Lookout to Elmira, New York City Harbor, and other points north.

In the end, the raid temporarily boosted Confederate morale while putting another dent in the morale of the Northern war populace. Overall, though, the outcome of the Johnson-Gilmor raid was negligible. Besides creating a temporary headache—to Confederate cavalrymen tasting ice cream for the first time, to the local populace, and to Union authorities—the raid was just a small disturbance during Early's invasion.

The initial reasoning behind the raid showed the desperation of—and imagination of—the Confederate high command to reverse the tide of war in 1864. However, the entire mission indeed proved "utterly impossible for man or horse to accomplish."

PHILLIP GREENWALT *is a supervisory ranger with the National Park Service. He is co-author of three books in the ECW Series and co-founder of Emerging Revolutionary War.*

WELCOME
BOROUGH
OF
CHAMBERSBURG
Incorporated 1803

BURNING OF CHAMBERSBUR

Occupied the morn
July 30, 1864, by
of Confederate Ger
McCausland. Failing
tain ransom, he bur
town in reprisal f
in the Shenandoah
by Gen. David Hur

PENNSYLVANIA HISTORICAL AND MUSEUM C

McCausland's Raid and the Burning of Chambersburg

APPENDIX E
BY AVERY C. LENTZ

During the initial months of the summer campaign in the Shenandoah Valley, Union Gen. David Hunter's forces had been especially destructive to Southern property—including many private residences of Confederate political officials and, more famously, the Virginia Military Institute in Lexington, Virginia. As a result, his counterpart—Lt. Gen. Jubal Early—vowed that the Northern people would likewise know the price of the war and how horrible it could be.

During Early's campaign in Maryland, he demanded ransom from many large cities and towns—such as Hagerstown and Frederick. As his forces withdrew in late July, Early set his sights on another Northern town which had been a significant locale during previous invasions: the town of Chambersburg, Pennsylvania.

To make the raid, Gen. Early selected Brig. Gen. John McCausland to lead a force north of the Mason-Dixon line to Chambersburg. Early ordered McCausland to ransom the town for a sum of $100,000 in gold or $500,000 in greenbacks; if the town could not meet those demands, they would face the consequences. Early also made it clear that McCausland was to return immediately south to rejoin the army as soon as possible afterwards.

When McCausland received his orders on July 28, 1864, he was summoned to General Early's headquarters in Martinsburg, West Virginia. By his own account, McCausland "nearly fell out of the saddle when he read the orders" and "did not agree with General Early's way of conducting war" for he preferred to follow Gen. Lee's example during the Gettysburg campaign. As the story of Chambersburg has been told over the decades, there has been dispute between Generals Early and McCausland over what justified the raid to Chambersburg and who had the last say in the decision to burn the town. Seeing as both men made allegations against each other at the beginning of the 20th century when they were approaching their deaths, it is still unclear who is right or wrong.

A historic marker—one of several in the Chambersburg town square—recounts the burning of the town in the summer of 1864. (cm)

Regardless, Early ordered McCausland to head north with his brigade of 1,400 cavalry troopers—the 14th, 16th, 17th, and 22nd Virginia Cavalry regiments—along with the two ordnance rifles of T. E. Jackson's Company and the two smoothbores of J. H. McClanahan's Company of the Horse Artillery.

McCausland was also informed that his unit would not be conducting this raid alone. They were to meet up with Brig. Gen. Bradley T. Johnson's Confederate cavalry brigade at Hammond's Mill, Virginia, on July 28 and proceed north across the Potomac River and into Maryland and Pennsylvania.

Johnson was a native of Frederick and had served as a delegate at the National Democratic Convention in Baltimore during the 1860 election before his delegation withdrew from the convention and united with a faction of Southern Whigs who supported Breckenridge for president during that election. Being a Confederate sympathizer, Johnson went on to form a company of the Confederate 1st Maryland Infantry. By 1864, he was commanding a cavalry force of 1,400 men in Early's army.

Johnson's force consisted of the 1st and 2nd Maryland Cavalry regiments and 8th and 21st Virginia Cavalry regiments alongside the 27th, 36th, and 37th Virginia Cavalry

Chambersburg was no stranger to visits from either army. Confederate and Union soldiers—such as the Federals making camp in these church pews—had both been through the town the summer before. (loc)

battalions with two 3-inch ordnance rifles of the 2nd Maryland (Baltimore) Light Artillery. This gave McCausland an approximate total of 2,800 troopers and six cannon—a formidable force that had no substantial Union force in their path to obstruct them. Major General Darius Couch commanded the Federal Department of the Susquehanna during the summer of 1864, but he had mostly emergency militia infantry and cavalry regiments to resist hardened Confederate veterans that outnumbered and outgunned his forces immensely.

In other words, the odds of successfully defending Chambersburg from the Confederate raiders were extremely grim.

The raid commenced in the early afternoon of July 28, 1864, with Maj. Harry Gilmor's combined force of the 1st and 2nd Maryland Cavalry crossing the Potomac River at McCoy's Ferry on July 29 at approximately 5:00 a.m. Gilmor advanced to the Baltimore Pike and secured the road in both directions, and then headed west down the Cove Road to Cherry Run to serve as a rear guard once McCausland and Johnson's combined force advanced north towards Clear Spring, Maryland.

The first Union forces the Confederates encountered was a 21-man detachment of the 12th Pennsylvania Cavalry at Cherry Run, who were caught by surprise. All but three of the 21-man detachment were captured without firing a shot.

Another skirmish ignited at Clear Spring itself, where Maj. Shadrack Foley's 350-man force from the 14th Pennsylvania Cavalry made a gallant, yet futile charge at the bulk of the 1st Marylanders, arrayed in skirmish lines around the village. The 1st Maryland, joined by the 36th and 37th Virginia Cavalry battalions, easily checked the Pennsylvanians. Foley was forced to fall back down the Baltimore Pike towards Hagerstown where he set up a defensive position around Conococheague Creek. Gilmor pursued with detachments from the 1st Maryland, but were beaten back by Foley's troopers, who fought dismounted with Spencer repeating rifles in the underbrush along the creek. Gilmor's fell back to Clear Spring.

The main body of McCausland and Johnson's force began crossing the Potomac at McCoy's Ferry around 6 a.m. and continued to cross until 11 a.m. due to the number of men. In an effort to divert Union attention away from McCausland's raiders, Early sent the Confederate divisions of Robert Rodes and Stephen Ramseur near Williamsport, Maryland, where they crossed the river and began making a mock-advance toward Hagerstown to draw any Union force in the area away from McCausland.

After passing through Clear Spring, McCausland and Johnson's troopers advanced north into Pennsylvania toward the town of Mercersburg. After the main body of McCausland's force had passed through Clear Spring, Gilmor followed them as a rear guard, having suffered 17 casualties in the morning skirmish. The 36th Virginia Cavalry battalion led McCausland's raid north and again ran into Union resistance around the village of Shimpstown, Pennsylvania, at around 3 p.m. on July 29. The 45-man force was a detachment of Company F, 6th U.S. Cavalry under the command of Lt. Hancock T. McLean.

Unlike their comrades in the 14th Pennsylvania, McLean's men were veterans and had moved into the path of the massive Confederate force after coming from Carlisle, Pennsylvania, on July 26, and arriving in Chambersburg on the morning of the 27th. From Chambersburg, McLean swung his men to Mercersburg in the early morning of the 28th, where he sent a detachment of 15 men under a Lt. Jones to Shimpstown, where they set up a picket line.

The Union soldiers made contact with Virginia cavalrymen on the 29th, and McLean rushed the rest of his small force to confront the 200 men of the 36th Virginia Cavalry battalion. After a two-hour skirmish, McLean withdrew to St. Thomas, Pennsylvania, seven miles west of Chambersburg, where his forced was joined by a detachment from the 3rd U.S. Cavalry under Lt. Frank Stanwood.

By the evening of the 29th, McCausland and Johnson's troopers arrived in Mercersburg and began advancing toward Chambersburg as early as 11:30 p.m. More cavalry skirmishing erupted around 2 a.m. as McLean received aggressive skirmishing from McCausland's immediate force. Due to the night skirmish, McCausland did not push forward immediately until around 4:30 a.m., when daylight began to illuminate McLean's small force, and he was finally forced to open with canister fire. McLean's

The burning of the town looked almost apocalyptic to one sketch artist, who reproduced the scene for *Harper's Weekly*. (hw)

men then retreated through Chambersburg around 5 a.m. on the morning of July 30, to link up with the columns of Maj. Gen. William Averell's cavalry division as he pulled back from Greencastle all the way to Shippensburg. General Couch had evacuated his department headquarters from Chambersburg at 3 a.m. after the fighting at St. Thomas began, and then retired to the state capitol of Harrisburg.

By the time the Union forces were withdrawing from Chambersburg, McCausland held a meeting with General Johnson and his staff in the house of Henry Greenwault, a mile of west of town. McCausland relayed Early's orders to Johnson: the town was to be ransomed or burned to the ground.

At around 5:30 a.m., the two guns of the 2nd Maryland (Baltimore) Light Artillery fired a salute to announce the arrival of the Confederates in Chambersburg. Although the shells didn't cause any deaths or immediate damage to the area, one of the three shots struck the house of Jacob Eby on New England Hill, going through one window and passing out another on the opposite wall.

Around the same time, the Confederate troopers entered the downtown area of Chambersburg and began to disperse throughout the town itself. Many civilians were shocked when Confederates troopers barged into their shops and businesses to take whatever they wanted. Around 6:30 a.m., McCausland went to the Franklin Hotel for breakfast and did very little to control the "progress" his men were making through the town.

As soon as word leaked out about the ransom demands, the officials for the Bank of Chambersburg could not be found. Some civilians realized the gravity of their situation and tried to pay out of pocket, but the town as a whole was only able to amass about $50,000. When the ransom could not be met, McCausland ordered Johnson, who ordered Gilmor, to burn the town.

Squads of Confederate troopers spread out to fulfill the orders. "They would burst in the door with iron bars or [a] heavy plank, smash up any furniture with an ax, throw fluid or oil upon it, and apply the match," one observer recalled. A Confederate soldier remembered "the shrieks of women and children" and that "Cows, dogs, and cats were consumed" by the flames.

While the soldiers burned the town, they also looted extensively. Some, after entering homes, "would present pistols at the heads of inmates, men and women, and demand money or their lives." Brigadier General Bradley Johnson even criticized some of the Confederate troopers when he wrote, "Every crime in the catalog of infamy has been committed, I believe, except murder and rape." Johnson continued, "Highway robbery of watches and pocket-books was of ordinary occurrence."

Nearly 2,500 Chambersburg residents were affected by the plundering and destruction. A total of 278 residences and businesses, 98 barns and stables, and 173 outbuildings were destroyed. The losses totaled nearly $1.63 million dollars. Some reports

A memorial and fountain stand at the center of the Chambersburg town square as a testament to the town's compelling Civil War history. (cm)

say there were five free blacks who were kidnapped as contraband during the raid to be sold back into slavery, but no source can be found to support that claim. There is also no substantial record of any civilians being killed or wounded during the raid and burning. Major A. Caulder Bailey, the adjutant of the 8th Virginia Cavalry, was the only Confederate soldier killed during the incident. After the burning commenced, a drunken Bailey was shot dead by a bakery store owner after the officer became separated from the rest of his unit.

McCausland's force withdrew from Chambersburg around noon on July 30 while nearly one-third of the town remained in flames in the 88-degree heat. The Confederates soon headed back south into West Virginia by crossing the Potomac River at the McCoy's Ferry.

Upon hearing about the burning of Chambersburg, Union Maj. Gen. David Hunter reinforced General Averell's depleted forces with another cavalry division and sent the horse soldiers after the withdrawing Confederate raiders. Averell's forces eventually caught up with McCausland's and Johnson's forces at the town of Moorefield, West Virginia, on August 7. Averell's smaller force of 1,760 men surprised and smashed the combined force of 2,800 under McCausland. Federals captured more than 38 officers and 377 enlisted men, severely crippling the Confederate cavalry presence in the Shenandoah Valley for the rest of the war. It was considered the first instance of Union retaliation for the burning of Chambersburg, as many of the Confederates responsible were killed or captured at the battle of Moorefield.

Overall, the burning of Chambersburg was destructive, and many of the townspeople felt the Union high command was partially responsible for the incident since they did not protect them as well as they should have. However, Union forces—such as the Army of the Shenandoah under Maj. Gen. Philip Sheridan—used Chambersburg as a rallying cry as they wrought destruction through the Shenandoah Valley for the rest of the year.

AVERY LENTZ *graduated from Gettysburg College with a Bachelor's Degree in history and from Shippensburg University with a Master's Degree in applied history. He has worked as a park historian for Fredericksburg and Spotsylvania National Military Park and a guest services assistant for the National Museum of Civil War Medicine.*

The Literary Legacy of Lew Wallace

APPENDIX F
BY RYAN T. QUINT

It can generally be said for the commanders during the Civil War, that conflict became the defining feature of their lives. Some of them, of course, continued with prosperous lives after the war, and some, like Ulysses S. Grant and his acclaimed memoirs, published to great acclaim. None of them, however, reached the level of Lew Wallace. Tens of millions have read Wallace's works or seen famous film adaptions of the books, and for them, Wallace's Civil War experience is but little more than a footnote.

How is it that a general who fought one of the most important defensive stands of the entire war is more known for his literary works?

Wallace's interests in writing started in the wake of a devastating moment in life: the death of his mother when he was only seven years old. With his father serving as the governor of Indiana and later as a prominent judge, Wallace found himself largely left to his own devices. First he poured his energy into painting, but he was soon faced, as he later wrote, by his father who lectured, "I suppose you don't want to be a poor artist—poor in the sense of inability as well as poverty." Wallace nonetheless continued to draw and paint for his entire life—as evidenced by sketches done of the conspirators in the Lincoln Assassination trials, sketches that he drew to keep himself occupied in the more mundane moments—but as a young man, he needed to find a new vocation.

As one of Wallace's earliest biographers, Irvin McKee wrote, "now sixteen, [Wallace] turned to the novel." The teenaged Wallace threw himself into a project he entitled "The Man-At-Arms: A Tale of the Tenth Century," a project that, when he finished it, totaled some 250 pages of narrative. According to Wallace, "With respect to quality . . . was sophomoric; for the sentimentalism which ruled me in those days was of the fervid kind . . . the kind to keep a boyish imagination in lurid glow." The manuscript of the book, tucked away, "was somehow mislaid" and was never published.

As Wallace wrote "The Man-At-Arms," he also poured over the recently published *Conquest of Mexico* by William Prescott. Detailing Hernán Cortes's

Constructed by Wallace in 1895, this impressive building became his personal study. Today it is home to the General Lew Wallace Study & Museum. (loc)

Lew Wallace, much younger than most people are used to seeing him, at about 21 years old—around the same time he served during the Mexican War. By this point in his life, he had already started to experiment with novel writing, a road that would lead to *Ben-Hur.* (lw)

Robert Ingersoll, the famed agnostic who sat with Wallace on a train and discussed religion. Out of their conversation, Wallace set to re-examining perceptions about religion. Ingersoll had served in the Civil War as a colonel of cavalry and had even fought at Shiloh, the same battle that proved so troublesome for Wallace. Ingersoll died in 1899. (loc)

campaign against the Aztec civilization, Prescott's history captured Wallace's imagination, providing inspiration to the first work of Wallace's that would be published, *The Fair God.* Service as a young volunteer officer in the Mexican War in the 1840s gave Wallace a chance to see some of the sites he had read about in Prescott's book, and he added to and revised *The Fair God* throughout the 1850s and '60s, culminating with the book's publication in 1873.

The Fair God did moderately well for Wallace, but it was a train ride in 1876 that would fundamentally change his life, and that of American literature, forever. Making his way to a political convention in Indianapolis on an overnight train, Wallace was hailed by Robert Ingersoll. Ingersoll, a Civil War veteran like Wallace, invited Wallace to conversation, to which, as long as Ingersoll "let me dictate the subject," Wallace acquiesced.

Sitting down, Wallace asked, "Is there a God?" It was a question that the nationally famed agnostic Ingersoll, was probably readying himself for. Having filled lecture halls, Ingersoll had made a name for himself as one of the nation's most prominent thinkers on religion. A key point here is that Ingersoll identified as an agnostic, not an atheist, as he is sometimes misattributed. Looking to engage Wallace, Ingersoll answered the initial inquiry, and every one of Wallace's follow-ups with "I don't know: do you?" Playing the devil's advocate, Ingersoll sought to get Wallace thinking about a statement that Ingersoll went back to time and time again in his speeches on religion: "We do not know."

With all of Wallace's questions answered with another question, Ingersoll set into his argument. "He was," Wallace later wrote, "in prime mood; and beginning, his ideas turned to speech, flowing like a heated river." Two hours later, when the train arrived at Indianapolis, Ingersoll and Wallace separated, leaving Wallace bewildered by the agnostic's rhetoric.

"I was in a confusion of mind not unlike dazement," Wallace wrote later, recollecting his walk through Indianapolis's streets, almost in a trance. "Was [Ingersoll] right? What had I on which to answer yes or no? He had made me ashamed of my ignorance: and then . . . as I walked on in the cool darkness, I was aroused for the first time in my life to the importance of religion."

Wallace set himself on answering Ingersoll's questions.

The end result made him internationally famous: the 1880 publication of *Ben-Hur: A Tale of the Christ.*

Wallace had already started work on the novel while he served as the territorial governor of New Mexico years earlier, but the train ride with Ingersoll gave Wallace a renewed energy. With the protagonist Judah Ben-Hur, Wallace introduced the reader to the life of Jesus Christ; Ben-Hur's life of vengeance for being wrongly accused is replaced by forgiveness as the titular character continues to meet with Jesus. In writing his magnum opus, Wallace had his answer for Ingersoll, resulting in "a conviction amounting to absolute belief in God and the divinity of Christ."

Ben-Hur swept the United States within just two years of publication. Copies flew off the shelves, earning Wallace, by 1886, $11,000 annually in royalties. Within six years, *Ben-Hur* could barely be kept in stock, selling about 4,500 copies a month.

Ben-Hur made it into the hands of the nation's most powerful people and opened more paths of advancement for Wallace. On April 19, 1881, President of the United States James A. Garfield wrote a letter to Lew Wallace. Addressing his letter "Dear General," Garfield scribbled, "I have this morning finished reading *Ben-Hur* and I must thank you for the pleasure it has given me." Only a little more than a month into his administration, Garfield found himself overwhelmed by the rush of the presidency. "With this beautiful and reverent book you have lightened the burden of my daily life," he praised.

Garfield went further than just praising Wallace—he offered him a job. A jack-of-all trades similar to Wallace, Garfield wondered if a book similar to *Ben-Hur* and its teachings of Christianity could be done for Islam. With that as an objective,

A month into his administration, President James A. Garfield read *Ben-Hur* and worked to get a position for Wallace in the Ottoman Empire. On July 2, 1881, Garfield was shot by a mentally unstable Charles Guiteau and died on September 19, eleven weeks later. The railroad station Garfield was in when he was shot was later razed and is today the site of the West Building for the National Gallery of Art. During the Civil War, Garfield had served as Chief of Staff for William Rosecrans during the Chickamauga campaign in the fall of 1863. (loc)

The former president of the Confederacy, Jefferson Davis, read *Ben-Hur* and sat up through the night to finish it with his daughter. (loc)

Wallace found himself appointed as the ambassador to the Ottoman Empire. In 1885, at the end of his term, Wallace set himself to writing the book Garfield had envisioned. Wallace had published, in 1893, *The Prince of India: Or Why Constantinople Fell.* Garfield never got to the see the book, having been slain by an assassin's bullet (and questionable medical care) in 1881.

President Garfield was not the only noteworthy reader of *Ben-Hur.* Even prominent foes of Wallace's read his work, perhaps most notably Jefferson Davis, the former president of the Confederacy. By candlelight Davis and his daughter, Winnie, read the novel "until daybreak," but even that was not good enough for Davis, who "did not go to rest until he had finished it."

The Prince of India added to Wallace's bibliography, but did not prove to be as popular as *Ben-Hur.* By the end of the nineteenth century, *Ben-Hur* replaced Harriet Beecher Stowe's *Uncle Tom's Cabin* as the best-selling American novel of the century, and it held onto the title until the 1930s when it was replaced by Margaret Mitchell's *Gone with the Wind.*

Ben-Hur proved an easy choice to be adapted to the screen, and film producers clamored for the rights to Wallace's creation. In 1924 producers got the rights to *Ben-Hur* for the astronomical sum of $600,000 (equivalent of $10 million in 2008), and the ensuing silent film cost another $3.9 million to bring the epic to life. More famously, in 1959, with Charlton Heston in the lead role, audiences were reintroduced to Judah Ben-Hur in one of the most successful films of the twentieth century. A 2016 big-budget remake introduced twenty-first century moviegoers to the character.

Retiring to Crawfordsville, Wallace lived out the rest of his life, writing to the very end. His massive two-volume *Autobiography* was still unfinished when he died in 1905. Looking over his pages to finish it for him posthumously, Wallace's wife Susan found the last section he had written about: the battle of Monocacy.

A poster for the 1959 film adaption of *Ben-Hur* starring Charlton Heston. Costing more than $15 million, the epic became famous for its scenes depicting the climatic chariot race and naval battles. The film easily recouped its production costs and is ranked 72nd on the list of the American Film Institute's Top 100 Great American Films. (loc)

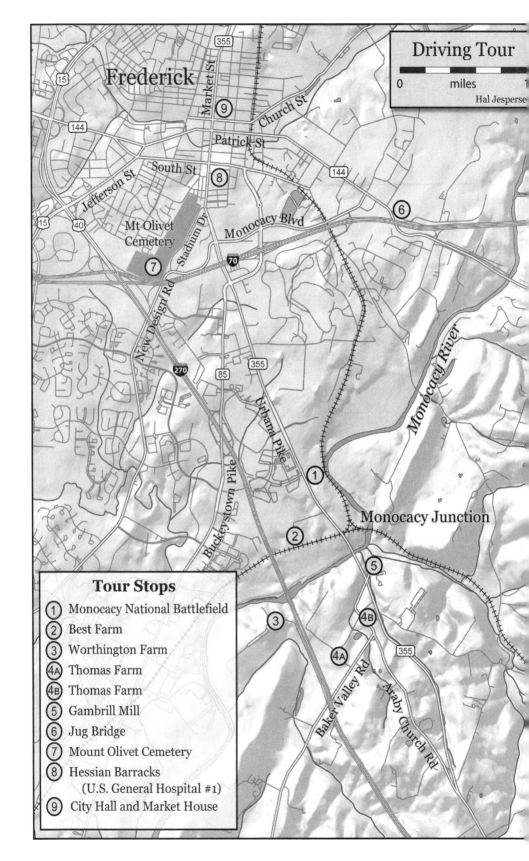

Driving Tour

0   miles   1

Hal Jespersen

Frederick

Market St

Church St

Patrick St

South St

Jefferson St

Mt Olivet Cemetery

Stadium Dr

Monocacy Blvd

Monocacy River

New Design Rd

Urbana Pike

Buckeystown Pike

Monocacy Junction

Baker Valley Rd

Araby Church Rd

Tour Stops
① Monocacy National Battlefield
② Best Farm
③ Worthington Farm
④ⒶThomas Farm
④ⒷThomas Farm
⑤ Gambrill Mill
⑥ Jug Bridge
⑦ Mount Olivet Cemetery
⑧ Hessian Barracks
   (U.S. General Hospital #1)
⑨ City Hall and Market House

Touring the Battlefield

The best place to start touring the Monocacy battlefield is at the National Park Service Visitor Center, located at 5201 Urbana Pike, Frederick, Maryland 21704. Visitors should pick up one of the park's maps. This book does repeat some of the park's stops, but it adds some of its own, as well. Inside the visitor center on the ground floor are rest rooms, a water fountain, and a bookstore. An excellent gallery upstairs includes a fiber-optics map that portrays the fighting on July 9, 1864.

GPS: 39°22'625" N, 77°23'737" W

⟶▶ TOUR STOP 1: **Monocacy Battlefield Visitor Center**

This area looks much the same as it did in 1864: open, rolling countryside. On July 9, 1864, this became the staging area for Maj. Gen. Stephen D. Ramseur's division of Confederate infantry for its attacks against the Federal skirmish line that took shelter near the Monocacy Junction of the Baltimore & Ohio Railroad. The single cannon next to the visitor center approximately marks the location of some of the artillery belonging to Lt. Col. William Nelson, whose battalion included the first Confederate cannons to fire during the battle. Leading from the parking lot is a quick loop trail that brings you down to the location of the Federal skirmish line along the railroad tracks. Please do not cross the railroad tracks as the line is still very active with freight trains.

In your car, turn left onto the Urbana Pike and drive 0.31 miles. Turn to your right onto the National Park access road to the Best farm. Follow the road to the parking area.

GPS: 39°22'14'1" N, 77°23'55'0" W

⟶▶ TOUR STOP 2: **Best Farm**

The main home of the Best farm dates to the very late eighteenth century

Opened in 2007 to replace a previous contact station, the Monocacy National Battlefield Visitor Center is the best place to start one's trip around the battlefield. Exhibits such as Lew Wallace's coat (right) adorn the walls. (cm)(cm)

and was owned by the Vincendiere family—French refugees who fled Saint-Domingue (modern Haiti) during the Haitian Revolution. Settling outside of Frederick, the Vincendieres named their home *L'Hermitage*. They brought along some of their slaves from Haiti, and evidence points to the Vincendieres as being ruthless slave masters—a man traveling by the property in the early nineteenth century wrote that, from the Georgetown Pike (modern Urbana Pike) he could see "farm instruments of torture, stocks, whips, etc." The National Park Service has recently, through archaeology, unearthed a row of slave houses near the Urbana Pike.

During the Civil War, the Best family lived on the property, from whom it gets its name today, but they did not own the land or home; rather, they rented from Charles E. Trail, who lived in nearby Frederick. In 1862, during the Maryland campaign that culminated at the battle of Antietam, a copy of Gen. Robert E. Lee's Special Orders 191 were lost on the Best farm and subsequently discovered by Union soldiers from the 27th Indiana Infantry.

On July 9, 1864, Confederates used the Best farm as both an emplacement for artillery pieces as

Originally constructed in the late eighteenth century, the home once known as *L'Hermitage* has gone through several additions and stages. In 1864 when Union and Confederate forces clashed, the building seen above was not united, but was rather two separate structures—one the main home and the second a kitchen. (cm)

well as a nest for sharpshooters. The cannon near the main home represents a section of Cpt. John Massie's Fluvanna Artillery. Union gunners in the Baltimore Light Artillery opened fire on the Confederate sharpshooters located on the Best farm, burning down a barn (see Chapter Seven).

Follow the park access road back to the Urbana Pike and turn right. Continue on the Urbana Pike for 0.6 miles and then turn right onto Araby Church Road. Drive for 0.45 miles, and then turn right onto Baker Valley Road. Continue on Baker Valley Road for 0.64 miles and then, directly after the I-270 overpass, turn right onto the National Park Access Road for the Worthington farm. Follow the road to the parking area.

GPS: 39°21'42.0" N, 77°24'06.0" W

▶ TOUR STOP 3: **Worthington Farm**

Clifton, the home of the Worthington family, played a vital role in the battle of Monocacy. The brick home was constructed in 1851, but the Worthington family did not move in until 1862. During the battle of Monocacy, most of the Worthington family—including the battle's first historian, Glenn Worthington, who was six years old at the time— took cover in the basement of the home.

A loop trail brings you from Clifton down to the banks of the Monocacy in the general area of the Worthington-McKinney Ford, which was used first by Confederate cavalry, then Confederate infantry, to get across the Monocacy River. The exact location of the ford has been obscured over time as the Monocacy River goes through its geological evolutions.

During the climatic episode of the battle—Maj. Gen. John Gordon's attack—his superior, Maj. Gen. John Breckinridge, made his headquarters in Clifton's front yard. After the battle, wounded were gathered near Clifton before being treated for their wounds.

The cannon next to the home marks the location of the Monroe Artillery, commanded by Maj. William McLaughlin, which supported Gordon's attack in the afternoon of July 9, 1864.

Follow the access road back to the Baker Valley Road. Turn left onto the Baker

The Worthington family had only lived in their home for about two years when the armies came to battle in July 1864. (cm)

Valley Road and drive for 0.33 miles, and then turn left into the parking area for Thomas Farm A.

GPS: 39°21'26.1" N, 77°23'28.1" W

⟶ TOUR STOP 4: Thomas Farm A

Known as "Araby," the main brick home was built circa 1780, making it the oldest extant building on the preserved portion of the battlefield. Christian Keefer Thomas bought the property in 1860 and owned it through the Civil War.

In late June 1863, the Army of the Potomac came through Frederick on its way to destiny at the battle of Gettysburg in early July. Over the course of three days, Araby acted as the headquarters for Maj. Gen. Winfield S. Hancock, commanding the II Corps.

A year later, Araby saw the climax of the battle of Monocacy. First, the property line between the Worthington and Thomas farms was the scene of Brig. Gen. John McCausland's repulse around noontime (see Chapter Seven), and then Araby saw Maj. Gen. John Gordon's bloody attack in the afternoon (see Chapter Nine). During McCausland's second attack as well as during Gordon's advance, the Thomas farm stood in the midst of the bullets and artillery shrapnel, and still bears the scars of combat today.

A series of trails leads around the Thomas farm. One of those trails, the Middle Ford Trail, brings you down toward the river, near where a rope ferry operated until the 1830s. Also visible on these trails are the road traces used by Federal soldiers for protection during Gordon's attack.

The Thomas farm hosts National Park Service administrative offices today, and the building is closed to the public except for special occasions.

The fighting surged back and forth around the Thomas farm: First held by Federal forces, then pushed out by John McCausland's troopers, then a Union counter-attack, and finally the climax with John B. Gordon's division of Confederate troops. Here around Araby fell the most casualties of the battle. A walking trail, marked with blue arrows, curls around the property, covering the space that Gordon's men attacked over. (rq)(cm)

Once finished with the Middle Ford and other trails, return to your car. Take a left onto Baker Valley Road and drive straight to the intersection of Baker Valley Road and Araby Church Road. Turn left onto Araby Church Road, and then turn into the gravel pull-off maintained by the National Park Service.

GPS: 39°21'41.7" N, 77°23'16.9" W

⟶ Tour Stop 5: Thomas Farm B

This was the location of James Rickets's last line of defense after having been pushed from the grounds of the Thomas farm. In the sunken cut of the Georgetown Pike, Ricketts's men fired into John Gordon's division before being outflanked on the right by William Terry's Virginians. The Georgetown Pike was altered to its current form in the Urbana Pike after the Civil War.

A National Park Service wayside sign tells the story of the final push against the Federal forces inside the cut of the Georgetown Pike. (cm)

Two nearby monuments—one to Pennsylvania state forces and one to the 10th Vermont Infantry—mark the Federal line. The 10th Vermont held the left flank of Lew Wallace's entire infantry force during the battle of Monocacy.

A month after the battle of Monocacy, in August 1864, the Thomas farm also served as the host site for a meeting of Union generals that included Ulysses S. Grant, Philip Sheridan, James B. Ricketts, and others, who had come to the Monocacy Junction to plan their next offensive.

Drive back to the intersection of Araby Church Road and the Urbana Pike (M-355). At the stop sign, drive straight across the Urbana Pike into the parking area for the Gambrill Mill.

GPS: 39°22'02.5" N, 77°23'14.7" W

⟶ Tour Stop 6: Gambrill Mill

The Gambrill Mill marked the center of Lew Wallace's battle line on July 9, 1864. Troops near the mill were drawing rations when the first Confederate artillery shells landed home, marking the commencement of the battle.

A short trail brings you down to the Monocacy River. The bridge for vehicular use on the Urbana Pike is constructed near the site of the wooden covered bridge that burned during battle. Also visible is a railroad bridge; this modern bridge is constructed on the same site as the Baltimore & Ohio Railroad

A walking trail at the Gambrill Mill brings one down to the Monocacy River where the railroad bridge is visible as well as the Urbana Pike truss over the river—the original site of the wooden covered bridge. (cm)

Bridge—the bridge B&O President John W. Garrett so intensely wanted defended. During the battle, Federal skirmishers were forced to scramble over the railroad ties after the wooden bridge was burned to prevent its capture (see Chapter Ten).

The Gambrill Mill served as the National Park Service's visitor center before the construction of the new center (Stop 1) in 2006. Originally two stories, the mill has been adapted over time. Behind the mill, on a small ridge, is a large home, architecturally in the Second Empire style, built by the Gambrill family in 1872. The Gambrills called the home Edgewood, but later owners of the home called it Boscobel.

In your car, turn right onto the Urbana Pike. Drive for 2.78 miles until getting to the intersection of the Urbana Pike and Monocacy Boulevard. Turn right onto Monocacy Boulevard. Drive on Monocacy Boulevard for 1.29 miles, and then turn right onto East Patrick Street (M-144). Drive on East Patrick Street for 0.16 miles. The road will fork, with opposite-direction one-way travel on the left while East Patrick Street continues on the right with a cut-through. Turn left onto the cut-through, and then right. Immediately after turning right, turn right again into the parking space for the Jug Bridge.

GPS: 39°24'18.3" N, 77°23'01.1" W

⟶ TOUR STOP 7: Jug Bridge

The Stone Bridge over the Baltimore Pike, defended by Brig. Gen Erastus Tyler during the battle of Monocacy, no longer exists. However, this "jug" did sit atop the bridge for decades, even witnessing the Marquis de Lafayette's 1824 return trip to the United States. Rumor tells that a cask of whiskey was housed within the larger stone jug.

The area you are in now, extremely chaotic with traffic, in 1864 was rural countryside. This area was occupied Maj. Gen. Robert Rodes's Confederate division. While the majority of the division stayed behind, Rodes deployed sharpshooters near here to engage with Tyler's men (see Chapter Six).

Turn left onto East Patrick Street. Drive 0.23 miles to Monocacy Boulevard and turn left. You are now re-tracing the route you took to get to the Jug Bridge. Drive on Monocacy Boulevard for 1.29 miles back to the Urbana Pike. Turn right onto Urbana Pike and drive for 0.27 miles and then turn left into the entrance of Mt. Olivet Cemetery. The cemetery has two brick columns on each side of the entrance and, facing the street, has a black iron fence.

GPS: 39°24'23.0" N, 77°24'44.3" W

Though the stone bridge defended by Erastus Tyler's Federals no longer exists, the "jug" that gave the bridge the nickname "Jug Bridge" still does. The name comes from a popular telling, likely apocryphal, that at one time a cask of whiskey sat inside the jug. (cm)

While stopping to see the jug, also notice the monument to the Marquis de Lafayette, a prominent French soldier who fought for the fledgling United States during the American Revolution. Lafayette made a return trip to the United States in 1824, where he was heralded as a hero and welcomed by thousands of grateful citizens, including at Frederick. (cm)

Tour Stop 8: Mount Olivet Cemetery

Frederick's most famous burial ground, Mount Olivet is home today to such luminaries as Francis Scott Key, who authored what would become "The Star Spangled Banner" while he watched the bombardment of Fort McHenry at Baltimore in 1814. Also buried here is Barbara Fritchie, a Frederick native who was made famous in an 1862 poem that purported her to flaunt an American flag in the face of "Stonewall" Jackson when the Confederates marched through Frederick in the fall of 1862. Glenn H. Worthington, the battle of Monocacy's first historian, is also buried here.

More central to this book's narrative, Mount Olivet also contains the resting place for hundreds of the Confederate dead from the battle of Monocacy.

For readers interested in seeing the resting place for the

A monument to Francis Scott Key, the most famous internment in Mt. Olivet Cemetery, dominates the cemetery's main entrance. Key wrote "The Star Spangled Banner," which became the national anthem by Congressional declaration on March 3, 1931. (cm)

The fifteen-foot high statue memorializing Confederate soldiers in Mount Olivet Cemetery (left) was unveiled in 1881 and constructed using Italian marble atop a granite platform. Conversely, the monument honoring Union dead, including those killed at Monocacy, at the Antietam National Cemetery (right), was unveiled in 1880 and weighs a grand total of 250 tons. (cm)(rq)

Union dead from the battle of Monocacy, you will need to drive to the Antietam National Cemetery. Originally buried on the battlefield or at nearby hospitals, Union soldiers were re-interred in the National Cemetery in post-war years.

Turn left onto Urbana Pike, which in downtown Frederick is also called South Market Street. Drive for 0.233 miles and street park on South Market Street. Walk onto the campus of the Maryland School for the Deaf, which, during the pre-Civil War years, was known as the Hessian Barrack. During the Civil War, it was the site of U.S. General Hospital # 1.

GPS: 39° 24'539" N, 77° 24'578" W

⟶ **TOUR STOP 9: Hessian Barracks (U.S. General Hospital #1)**

Constructed to house Hessian prisoners of war during the American Revolution, the buildings here are now home to the Maryland School for the Deaf. Of the original barracks, only the eastern barrack remains. In the aftermath of the battles of Antietam and Monocacy, this site was used as a Union hospital to care for thousands of wounded soldiers (See Appendix B).

A soldier in the 151st New York Infantry became separated from his regiment during the battle of Monocacy and subsequently was detailed as a nurse at this hospital. "I am alone to wait on fifty or sixty patients, so you may judge how much time I have to write," he quickly jotted a little over a week

Today on the campus for the Maryland School for the Deaf, this lone building is all that survives of the once-large complex for the Hessian Barracks, or General Hospital #1. Hundreds of wounded from the battle of Monocacy filtered through here. (rq)

after the battle. About a month later, the soldier wrote on the progression of the wounded men: "Limbs that were taken off when they were first wounded are getting along nicely. A good many lose their lives because the doctors try to save the limb. If I am ever wounded in the joints, I will tell the doctors to saw it off at once." (This contrasts starkly with the stereotypical-but-inaccurate depiction of Civil War doctors being incompetent butchers.)

From here, you have two choices. You can leave your car parked in its space and walk into town for the remaining stop, or you can drive there. Both follow the same directions, but street parking can be a scarcity in downtown Frederick.

Turn right, back onto Urbana Pike (South Market Street). Go straight for 0.45 miles, advancing through Frederick. In the middle of the block between West Church Street and West 2nd Street, is the final stop of the tour on the right side, the former City Hall and Market House, now the site of a popular Frederick restaurant.

GPS: 39°24'57.8" N, 77°24'38.3" W

TOUR STOP 10: City Hall and Market House—Where Frederick's Ransom was demanded

This was the site of Frederick's City Hall and Market House during the Civil War, though the present building dates to 1873. On July 9, 1864, Lt. Gen. Jubal Early issued a ransom for $200,000 from Frederick's town leaders. If the demand were not paid, Early threatened to burn the town. After first delaying and refusing to pay the ransom, the city's leaders turned to Frederick banks in the wake of the Federal defeat.

The building that exists today was not built until the 1870s. But on July 9, 1864, it was here that Jubal Early's demand for a $200,000 ransom was delivered to Frederick's market house. Though they originally resisted, the town's leaders capitulated when it became clear that Lew Wallace was going to lose the battle. (jw)

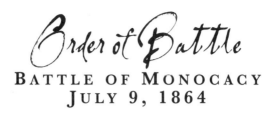

BATTLE OF MONOCACY
JULY 9, 1864

MIDDLE DEPARTMENT / VIII CORPS
Maj. Gen. Lew Wallace

First Separate Brigade: Brig. Gen. Erastus Tyler
1st Maryland Potomac Home Brigade • 3rd Maryland Potomac Home Brigade
11th Maryland Infantry • 144th Ohio National Guard • 149th Ohio National Guard

CAVALRY: Lt. Col. David R. Clendenin
8th Illinois Cavalry • 159th Ohio Mounted Infantry • "Mixed Cavalry" and Loudoun Rangers

ARTILLERY
Baltimore Light Artillery • 8th New York Heavy Artillery (Detachment)

VI CORPS, ARMY OF THE POTOMAC (Detachment)
THIRD DIVISION: Brig. Gen. James Ricketts
First Brigade: Col. William S. Truex
10th Vermont • 14th New Jersey • 106th New York • 151st New York • 87th Pennsylvania

Second Brigade: Col. Matthew R. McClennan
9th New York Heavy Artillery • 110th Ohio • 122nd Ohio • 126th Ohio
138th Pennsylvania

ARMY OF THE VALLEY DISTRICT
Lt. Gen. Jubal A. Early

BRECKINRIDGE'S CORPS: Maj. Gen. John C. Breckinridge
GORDON'S DIVISION: Maj. Gen. John B. Gordon

Evans's Brigade: Brig. Gen. Clement Evans (w), Col. Edmund Atkinson
*13th Georgia • 26th Georgia • 31st Georgia • 38th Georgia • 60th Georgia
61st Georgia • 12th Georgia Battalion*

York's Brigade: Brig. Gen. Zebulon York (This brigade consolidated the
Louisiana Regiments from Harry Hays's Brigade and Leroy Stafford's Brigade—
both of which had taken heavy casualties in the Overland Campaign.)
*1st Louisiana • 2nd Louisiana • 5th Louisiana • 6th Louisiana • 7th Louisiana
8th Louisiana • 9th Louisiana • 10th Louisiana • 14th Louisiana • 15th Louisiana*

Terry's Brigade: Brig. Gen. William R. Terry
(This brigade consolidated the Virginia Regiments from the Stonewall
Brigade, John Jones's Brigade, and George Steuart's Brigade in the aftermath
of the Overland Campaign.)
*2nd, 4th, 5th, 27th, 33rd Virginia Consolidated Regiments • 21st, 25th, 42nd, 44th, 48th,
50th Virginia Consolidated Regiments • 10th, 23rd, 37th, Virginia Consolidated Regiments*

ECHOLS'S DIVISION: Brig. Gen. John Echols
Echols's Brigade: Col. George S. Patton
22nd Virginia • 25th Virginia • 23rd Virginia Battalion • 26th Virginia Battalion

Wharton's Brigade: Brig. Gen. Gabriel C. Wharton
45th Virginia • 51st Virginia • 30th Virginia Battalion

Smith's Brigade: Col. Thomas Smith
36th Virginia • 60th Virginia • 45th Virginia Battalion • Thomas's Legion

Vaughn's Brigade: Brig. Gen. John C. Vaughn
*1st Tennessee Cavalry • 39th Tennessee Mounted Infantry • 43rd Tennessee Mounted
Infantry • 59th Tennessee Mounted Infantry • 12th Tennessee Cavalry Battalion
16th Tennessee Cavalry Battalion • 16th Georgia Cavalry Battalion*

INDEPENDENT DIVISIONS (NO CORPS STRUCTURE)
RODE'S DIVISION: Maj. Gen. Robert Rodes
Grimes's Brigade: Brig. Gen. Bryan Grimes
*2nd North Carolina Battalion • 32nd North Carolina • 43rd North Carolina
45th North Carolina • 53rd North Carolina*

Cook's Brigade: Col. Philip Cook
4th Georgia • 12th Georgia • 21st Georgia • 44th Georgia

Cox's Brigade: Brig. Gen. William Cox
*1st North Carolina • 2nd North Carolina • 4th North Carolina • 14th North Carolina
30th North Carolina*

Battle's Brigade: Col. Charles Pickens
3rd Alabama • 5th Alabama • 6th Alabama • 12th Alabama • 61st Alabama

RAMSEUR'S DIVISION: Maj. Gen. Stephen D. Ramseur
Lilley's Brigade: Brig. Gen. Robert Lilley
13th Virginia • 31st Virginia • 49th Virginia • 52nd Virginia • 58th Virginia

Johnston's Brigade: Brig. Gen. Robert D. Johnston
5th North Carolina • 12th North Carolina • 20th North Carolina • 23rd North Carolina

Lewis's Brigade: Brig. Gen. William G. Lewis
6th North Carolina • 21st North Carolina • 54th North Carolina • 57th North Carolina

ARTILLERY: Brig. Gen. Armistead Long
Nelson's Battalion: Lt. Col. William Nelson
Milledge Georgia Artillery • Amherst Virginia Artillery • Fluvanna Virginia Artillery

Braxton's Battalion: Lt. Col. Carter Braxton
Allegheny Virginia Artillery • Stafford Virginia Artillery • Lee Virginia Artillery

McLaughlin's Battalion: Lt. Col. J. Floyd King
Lewisburg Virginia Artillery • Wise Legion Artillery • Monroe Virginia Artillery

CAVALRY: Maj. Gen. Robert Ransom
McCausland's Brigade: Brig. Gen. John McCausland
*14th Virginia Cavalry Regiment • 16th Virginia Cavalry Regiment
17th Virginia Cavalry • 22nd Virginia Cavalry Regiment*

Johnson's Brigade: Brig. Gen. Bradley T. Johnson
*8th Virginia Cavalry • 21st Virginia Cavalry • 34th Virginia Cavalry Battalion
36th Virginia Cavalry Battalion • 1st Maryland Cavalry • 2nd Maryland Cavalry Battalion*

Confederate dead, killed at Monocacy, line one of the walls of Frederick's Mt. Olivet Cemetery. (cm)

Suggested Reading

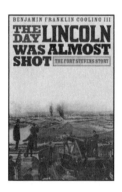

The Day Lincoln Was Almost Shot: The Fort Stevens Story
Benjamin Franklin Cooling III
Scarecrow Press (2013)
ISBN-13: 978-0810886223

Benjamin F. Cooling is one of the leading experts on
Jubal Early's 1864 invasion, and he wrote this book
in preparation of the 150th Anniversary of the battle
of Fort Stevens. For any readers interested in more
details about the battle fought at the doorstep of
Washington, D.C., where even President Abraham
Lincoln was a target, this is the book.

Bloody Autumn: The Shenandoah Valley Campaign of 1864
Daniel T. Davis and Phillip S. Greenwalt
Savas Beatie (2014)
ISBN-13: 978-1611211658

What happened after Jubal Early retreated across the
Potomac River on July 14, 1864? This installment in
the Emerging Civil War Series answers that question,
narrating the Shenandoah Valley Campaign,
including the Third Battle of Winchester, Fisher's
Hill, Tom's Brook, and Cedar Creek.

Last Chance for Victory: Jubal Early's 1864 Maryland Invasion
Brett W. Spaulding
Thomas Books (2010)
ISBN-13: 978-1577471523

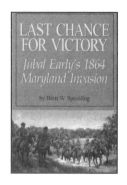

The best book for those looking for an in-the-weeds study of the tactical movements during the battle. Spaulding's study also contains a narrative for the Johnson-Gilmor Raid and the battle of Fort Stevens.

Shadow of Shiloh: Major General Lew Wallace in the Civil War
Gail Stephens
Indiana Historical Society (2010)
ISBN-13: 978-0871952875

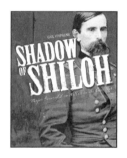

It is difficult to imagine a better biography of Lew Wallace than Stephens's being written for a long, long time. Stephens's biography of Wallace focuses on his service during the Civil War, specifically his actions at Shiloh and his subsequent efforts to clear his name of any wrongdoings. Wallace's decision to fight at Monocacy also features prominently.

Fighting for Time: The Battle of Monocacy
Glenn H. Worthington
1932; Reprinted by White Mane Publishing Co., Inc. (1985)
ISBN-13: 978-0942597714

Worthington's book was the premiere history published of the battle and should be read by anyone interested in Monocacy. As a young boy Worthington watched the battle from his family's basement.

About the Author

Ryan T. Quint has a degree in history from the University of Mary Washington. He is a seasonal National Park Ranger for the Fredericksburg & Spotsylvania National Military Park, as well as a guide at Historic Kenmore, the home of George Washington's sister, Betty Lewis. He writes for the blog Emerging Civil War (emergingcivilwar.com) and lives in Fredericksburg, Virginia.

(lm)